Overcoming Anxiety

Comments from leaders

Anxiety disorders are the number one mental health problem in the world and the only real and lasting answer is eternal life in Christ. Ken and Carolee have learned to cast their anxiety upon Christ and live fearlessly by faith, and have helped many others do the same, which is why I recommend this book.

Dr. Neil T. Anderson,
Founder and President Emeritus,
Freedom in Christ Ministries

Overcoming Anxiety is a fantastic and very usable handbook for dealing with the root issues and faulty thinking that lie behind our anxieties. It will give you straightforward, effective tools to help you apply the truths of God's Word to your specific situation. Expect your life to be changed for the better!

Steve Goss, Executive Director,
Freedom in Christ Ministries International

Overcoming Anxiety takes a down-to-earth, practical and applied approach to making use of scriptures in facing this big emotion. There are straightforward narratives from persons sharing about their daily struggles with anxiety and seeking to apply the scriptures. This is a unique feature of the book.

Dr. James Krahn, family practice

I was meeting with colleagues discussing how we might help those who have been struggling with ongoing chronic illness and pain. The consensus was, after much technical talk, that we need help in directing folks to a resource to give them hope and positive, practical advice on how to get back on the road to emotional health. I would wholeheartedly recommend this book to patients and practitioners alike.

Dr. Dennis Carrington, dentist

I find this book enjoyable and easy to use. I can pick it up for five minutes at a time and be encouraged. When I choose and write out some specific Bible verses on cards to leave where I will see them often, as it suggests, it helps me to remember God's presence during my day. Any book that helps me to have a closer relationship with the living God is a good book.

Dr. Sieg Hiebert

Comments from Readers

I didn't know I had a problem with anxiety. I think I had a way to hide it or cover it up even to myself. I am only just recognizing it now. Your book and materials are the key to getting set free. LH, business man

Thank you once again for this valuable tool. I do feel more at peace in my spirit since working in the book and reading the encouraging scriptures. MD, nurse

I've been going through the anchor verses ever since coming home to Nova Scotia. I've actually been meditating on one verse per day. It's been really good. Anxiety has been such a stronghold on my life and I really believe that this is the season to break those chains. Thank you so much for this book! AFD

Love your book! DC

I couldn't fall asleep last night so finally got up and read Anchor Verses. It worked. Bless you! M

I read the book and it ministered to me! I did the Anchor Verses for about 2 months and I really liked the focus and what it did to calm my spirits and focus totally on the Lord. FF, missionary

The book is on the way to Saskatoon. I would like another one. I can't seem to hang on to the book – it seems I feel others need it too. I think it is excellent! BC, music teacher

I want to thank you for the book. I have read through it and am finding the notion of Anchor Verses to be very helpful. The particular verses you chose are meaningful to me. DW, international humanitarian worker

I have read your book. It's excellent - very well done! I love the way you have pulled so many different things together to give people great tools to renew their minds. SG

Overcoming Anxiety

Anchored in the Word

Overcoming Anxiety

Anchored in the Word

a biblical resource
for those who are anxious
and for those who love them

Carolee and Ken Neufeld

Art Bookbindery
Winnipeg, MB R3H 0N1

Overcoming Anxiety

Anchored in the Word

Second printing, February 2018

The hymns quoted in this book are favourites that have been sung by God's people for generations. They are public domain and can be used without permission.

To protect the identity and privacy of individuals, some names of persons have been changed in stories, emails or casual references.

This second printing has small changes. It also includes an index of Bible references at the end.

Overcoming Anxiety

ISBN: 978-0-9959093-0-4

Art Bookbindery
Printed in Canada

Appreciation

We are deeply grateful to friends and family who have contributed to this book.

Evan Falk, Bonnie Falk, Lisa Epp and Daniel Epp each read the manuscript and gave very valuable suggestions. Both couples are serving overseas with Wycliffe Bible Translators.

Jennifer Kornelsen provided a watercolor painting for the cover design. Jennifer is our daughter and a pastor with Many Rooms Church Community in Winnipeg.

Joy Banks gave permission to include an image of one of her lino prints. Joy is a pastor at Grandview Calvary Baptist Church in Vancouver, British Columbia.

Connie Smith gave permission to use the words of her song "Always." Connie has written lyrics and composed music for many songs. She serves on a worship team at her church in southern Ontario.

John Neufeld gave permission to use his post that appeared on the church web-site. John is our son and lead pastor of The Meeting Place in Winnipeg, Manitoba.

"Jewels" was encouraged as she used the Anchor Verses which were then in the form of a 3-page hand out. She gave permission to include her reflections in this book.

"Ella" came through doubt and anxiety to a place of peace and clarity about a major decision. She gave permission for her story to be included in this book. She is now the mother of 2 children and places her confidence in the Lord.

Neil Anderson has had a big impact on our lives, as you can read on page 160. We are deeply grateful that he has affirmed us in writing this book on anxiety, which has its inspiration in his teaching, both in seminars and in his book *Finding Freedom from Fear.*

We thank God for all these contributors!

Carolee and Ken Neufeld

Using the Book

This book started a few years ago as a 3-page collection of what we dubbed Anchor Verses because they anchor our minds in what God says. *Overcoming Anxiety* is designed to be used, not just read. Steve Goss, Executive Director of Freedom in Christ Int., describes it as a *handbook*. So, have it at hand! Pick it up whenever you struggle with anxiety and find in it an encouragement, a reminder, or a strategy. Every page-spread is designed to stand on its own. Please also read the book from cover to cover so that you are familiar with the resources and prayers that you need for overcoming worry and fear.

It will be helpful for you to have a notebook or journal to use as you go through the book. For those who do not enjoy journaling, don't panic. The writing can be brief. You can choose any notebook for this or you may want to obtain the companion journal, available from Living Free Ministries.

What's Ahead?

Jesus says,

"Peace I leave with you;

my peace I give you.

I do not give to you

as the world gives.

1

Do not let your hearts

be troubled

and do not be afraid."

John 14:27

Worry, Fear and Anxiety

Fear and anxiety may have been with you for a long time and you are longing for peace.

Maybe you grew up in circumstances that caused constant stress and worry and you are carrying the tensions with you.

Perhaps worry and fear have come into your life because of something difficult or frightening that happened more recently.

No matter how or where it started, God is able to replace your worry, fear or anxiety with His amazing peace! Jesus Christ is the Living Word and he offers peace. The Bible is the written Word of God and it speaks peace!

Anchor Verses are the core of this book. These scripture truths will renew your mind (Romans 12:2) and give you hope. You will also find prayers and poetry, teaching and stories to guide your spiritual journey. We pray that the Holy Spirit will use these resources to encourage you.

The Lord your God is with you,

He is mighty to save.

He will take great delight in you;

He will quiet you with his love,

He will rejoice over you with singing.

Zephaniah 3:17 NIV '84

Why So Much Anxiety?

People often ask us, "Why is there so much anxiety around?" You may have wondered about that too.

Consider this

- families are in tatters
- movies are full of violence
- terrorism is ongoing
- cancer is a dreaded disease
- the economy is uncertain
- natural disasters are in the news daily
- personal problems abound

No wonder that fear and anxiety are increasing.

The Bible gives assurance of God's presence and love no matter what happens. Jesus is with us!

Peace be with You

The world bombards us with messages and images that escalate anxiety.

Jesus came to *give us life!*

"I have come that they may have life,
and have it to the full." John 10:10

Jesus came to *bring us wholeness!*

"...to proclaim freedom for the prisoners
and recovery of sight for the blind,
to set the oppressed free." Luke 4:18

Jesus came to *give us peace!*

"Peace be with you!" John 20:19

A Word from Ken and Carolee

introducing ourselves

We are a team! We clean the house together, we preach and teach together, we even write together! Naturally we each contribute our own gifts and interests. In cooking for example, Ken majors on the "B" words – breakfast, brunch, barbecue and bread. Carolee cooks main meals, and also makes a lot of tasty soups and African stews.

We have raised a big family and now it's a delight to have our kids and grandkids fill the backyard for a barbecue or an outdoor Thanksgiving feast. Or to have them home for Christmas dinner. Our life has also included public school teaching, camp directing, church planting and pastoral team ministry.

Our home is where we pray with people, host meals and meetings, do office work and love each other.

We both felt called to ministry at an early age. Ken remembers lining up his sister's dolls and preaching to them. Carolee recalls God stirring her heart at a missions conference when she was 16.

When we got married we anticipated a life of serving God together. Both of us have graduate degrees and are ordained. We have enjoyed living in northern Manitoba, in New Brunswick and in Winnipeg.

Since the early 1990's we have led Living Free workshops and seminars in many places and in a variety of denominations. Alongside the teaching we have had the opportunity to guide people in praying through personal and spiritual concerns in their lives.

It has been very rewarding to see women and men transformed by the Word of God and the power of the Holy Spirit.

A Personal Passion

Carolee's story

I am passionate about praying and using scripture to overcome fear. I know how it changed my life! I was restored to peace after I had traumatic experiences that resulted in extreme anxiety.

Late one October night I was folding laundry. My children, ages two to fifteen, were all asleep and my husband, Ken, was out of town. There was a knock at the door and that knock led to an intense and complex situation with Lucinda, a young woman who was doing drugs and involved in the occult.

That night in my own house Lucinda tried to kill me with a knife. But God intervened and miraculously I was unharmed.

When I went to bed hours later, after a visit from the police, I wondered how I would sleep. God drew my attention to Psalm 4:8, (in KJV at the time). "I will both lay me down and sleep, for thou Lord only makest me dwell in safety." That verse became a pillow for my head and I went to sleep peacefully.

The next day a stranger showed up at our back door and before I could intervene, our seven-year-old son invited him in. This man knew Lucinda. He knew what had happened. And he lived nearby.

There were clues that he was not safe either so I told him he had to leave and to my great relief he turned and walked out. But from then on I lived in fear of being attacked. Sounds in our old house terrified me. Strangers terrified me. Knives terrified me.

As months slipped by, I could see I was becoming mentally unhealthy. In waking hours my mind was increasingly twisted with fear and anxiety. One day I asked God to give me specific scripture truths to help me. I also decided to face my fears head-on and stop avoiding situations that were anxiety-producing.

Prayerfully I put my trust in God. As I read my Bible I found seven special verses and embraced them with my whole heart. Gradually my mind became a peaceful place. The memory of the trauma is still vivid but does not carry anxiety. I thank God for delivering me from fear and from death. He brought healing into my life through his precious Word!

Fear, Good or Bad?

"Fear is the most basic instinct of every living creature," write Dr. Neil Anderson and Rich Miller in their book *Freedom from Fear, Overcoming Worry and Anxiety*. "Fear is the natural response when our physical safety and psychological well-being are threatened." [2]

Fear is an inner response God has given to us for our protection. However, our emotions can become unhealthy if we do not process a difficult experience appropriately. Worry, irrational fear and anxiety are variations of unhealthy fear.

Worry is allowing our mind to dwell on difficulties or troubles. *Fear* is an unpleasant emotion that we have about an immediate danger or problem, or it seems to be immediate. *Anxiety* is uneasiness and tension about something that *might* happen or *could* happen. The thought that grips us is, *"What if?"*

Some *symptoms* that accompany anxiety are feeling tired, problems with sleeping, difficulty concentrating, being irritable, finding it hard to relax, shortness of breath, rapid heart rate, racing thoughts, sweating, muscle tension, feeling overwhelmed, expecting to break down and cry.

What is Stealing your Joy?

Dr. David Jeremiah in W*hat Are You Afraid Of?*

When I ask, "What are you afraid of?" I'm asking, "What is it that immobilizes you? What is stealing your joy and destroying your hope? What is robbing you of sleep, night after night? What keeps you from living by faith and being a risk taker? What keeps you from giving your life wholly to God who wants nothing but the best for you?" [3]

In all my years of following Christ, studying the Bible and pastoring well-intentioned Christians, I have yet to find a fear for which God does not have an answer. And the reason is simple: God Himself is the answer to all our fears. [4]

The Many Faces of Anxiety

Anxiety is called a *disorder* when it interferes with normal living, studies, relationships, job, etc.

Generalized anxiety disorder is worrying constantly and often anticipating the worst. It tends to be accompanied by unpleasant physical symptoms.

A *panic attack* is a feeling of sudden terror, and it may include shortness of breath, pounding heart, chest pain, dizziness and excessive perspiration.

Obsessive compulsive disorder is having unwanted thoughts and actions that seem unstoppable.

Post-traumatic stress disorder is distress following a traumatic event. It often includes recurring memories, flashbacks, nightmares and ongoing anxiety.

A *phobia* is a strong fear of a specific situation or object.

Social anxiety is a fear (phobia) of social situations, including fear of being judged or criticized by others.

What a Friend We have in Jesus

What a friend we have in Jesus,
  All our sins and griefs to bear!
What a privilege to carry
  Everything to God in prayer!
O what peace we often forfeit,
  O what needless pain we bear,
All because we do not carry
  Everything to God in prayer. [5]

Are we weak and heavy laden,
  Cumbered with a load of care?
Precious Saviour, still our refuge,
  Take it to the Lord in prayer.
Do your friends despise, forsake you?
  Take it to the Lord in prayer!
In his arms He'll take and shield you;
  You will find a solace there. [6]

Joseph M. Scriven, 1855

Anchored in Christ

For some people, the thought of seeking help for anxiety and fear causes their anxiety to increase.

The good news is that God is ready to help us in those difficult times. When Jesus noticed the fear of his disciples He said, "Don't be afraid."

The early Christians had to face horrific persecution by the Romans. Many were tortured and died for their faith. During that fearful time the anchor became a secret symbol of Christ-followers. It may have been inspired by these words, *"We have this hope as an anchor for the soul, firm and secure"* Hebrews 6:19. The anchor symbol has been found on the tombstones of many early believers.

Artist Joy Banks has depicted Christ as the anchor in her thought-provoking lino print. [7]

This picture of Christ the Anchor hangs in the roomy front entrance of our old house. It is a constant reminder that Jesus is our peace in the most stressful circumstances of life.

Christ the Anchor

Lino Print by Joy Banks

Used by Permission

Anchored or Anxious

Why is an anchor so important? In the world of ships and boats, the anchor keeps a vessel from drifting because of wind, waves or current.

We too have an anchor when worries and fears unsettle us or torment us. It's Jesus! He is with us. It's his Word, the Bible, that speaks to our minds and hearts. It restores peace and gives us hope.

All through the scriptures there are reminders and stories that show us how to trust God in difficult circumstances. However, there are times when the Bible may seem like just words on a page. Some people have said that to us.

How can the words of scripture transform? We invite you into an experiment. Would you commit just five to fifteen minutes a day over the next few weeks to thoughtfully and prayerfully read the Anchor Verses?

Up ahead you will find six clusters of Bible verses. Discover how God's Word will be your anchor to overcome worry, fear and anxiety. Keep reading to find out more.

Are You Anchored?

Will your anchor hold in the storms of life,
When the clouds unfold their wings of strife?
When the strong tides lift, and the cables strain,
Will your anchor drift or firm remain?

We have an anchor that keeps the soul
Steadfast and sure while the billows roll,
Fastened to the Rock which cannot move,
Grounded firm and deep in the Saviour's love. [8]

Priscilla Owens, 1882

> We have this hope as an anchor for the soul, firm and secure. Hebrews 6:19

Jewels

by Carolee

May I introduce Jewels? She has become a good friend. Jewels is a wife and also the mother of a young son. She has a satisfying career in the military.

In her life she has had many struggles; fear, worry and anxiety are among them. She called Living Free Ministries for help and that is how I got to know her. At one point she told me that what she appreciated and had been looking for was the kind of help that would push her to do something about the problems in her life.

Jewels accepted my challenge to try the Anchor Verses and as she used them she sent me her responses. With her permission I am sharing those emails. As you go through the six sections of Anchor Verses, you will read what she wrote to me.

I encourage you to personalize the verses as she has.

Carolee

The following email was written two months before Jewels started using the Anchor Verses.

Good morning Carolee,

If we as humans possessed such a thing as a "believe-o-meter" I would say mine is broken. I'm beginning to think that my problems are what I've created by not trusting God, and I'm struggling with trusting him because I still believe He is angry with me. I feel like it is an endless, repetitive sprint around the same mountain. I'm spiritually and emotionally tired, and I'm getting nowhere really fast. I feel like I've wasted your time over the last several months. I feel utterly useless as a person.

I love summer, but I'm not enjoying myself. I hope you are doing well.

Jewels

Trusting Jesus

Simply trusting every day,
Trusting through a stormy way;
Even when my faith is small,
Trusting Jesus, that is all.

Singing if my way is clear,
Praying if the path be drear;
If in danger for him call;
Trusting Jesus, that is all.

Trusting as the moments fly,
Trusting as the days go by;
Trusting him whate'er befall,
Trusting Jesus, that is all.

Edgar P. Stites, 1876

ANCHOR VERSES

for Overcoming

Worry, Fear

and Anxiety

9

Using the Anchor Verses Well

The *Anchor Verses* have been carefully chosen to calm your anxious heart. There are six sections and as you read a section a day you will grow in trusting God.

- Read *slowly* out loud. For the sake of flow, ignore the references.
- Read *thoughtfully*. Receive the truths as God's gift for you today and thank him for what He is saying to you. Use the first verse in each section (in **bold** print) as an opportunity for worship. The last verse of the section is **bold** for a strong finish.
- If you are able, *choose one verse* for the day. Don't agonize about this. Any verse is fine. Write out the verse and put it where you will see it often.

Some people who are anxious find themselves overwhelmed with following new instructions. If that is how you feel, take your first week to simply soak up the encouraging verses.

Note: Later, after you have gone through the Anchor Verses for the first time, you will find suggestions on how to make them even more helpful in your life.

Opposition

Be assured, there will be opposition as you start using the Anchor Verses. And it likely won't come from people.

Satan opposes God's Word. He does not want you to read it because he knows it will transform you. Jesus said, "The truth will set you free" (John 8:32).

The enemy does not want you to be free of anxiety. He wants to keep you in a cycle of fear and worry. In fact, he intends for it to become worse. Jesus tells us in John 10:10 that Satan is bent on destruction.

You may have thoughts like, "I can't do this because it's too hard to pick a verse for the day." Where are these thoughts coming from? The enemy knows that you will find peace as you absorb God's Word by reading it and by focusing on it throughout the day.

How do you overcome this opposition? According to James 4:7 and 8, you *submit yourself to God* and *resist the devil* in the name of Jesus Christ. Then *draw near* to God, in this case, by reading the Anchor Verses.

Support and Accountability

Enlisting the help of a friend will keep you going when you are inclined to be inconsistent with the Anchor Verses or to give up completely.

Think of somebody you trust who could be a support to you. If you are unsure, ask God to bring someone to mind.

Explain to that person what you intend to do. Ask whether they would be open to receiving brief emails from you and whether they would pray for you and give some encouragement. Be sure to put a limit on it. You could suggest, for example, once or twice through the Anchor Verses or 6 to 12 short emails.

After reading a section, send your accountability partner a few sentences on what you found helpful in the Anchor Verses.

Section One

GOD IS MY REFUGE

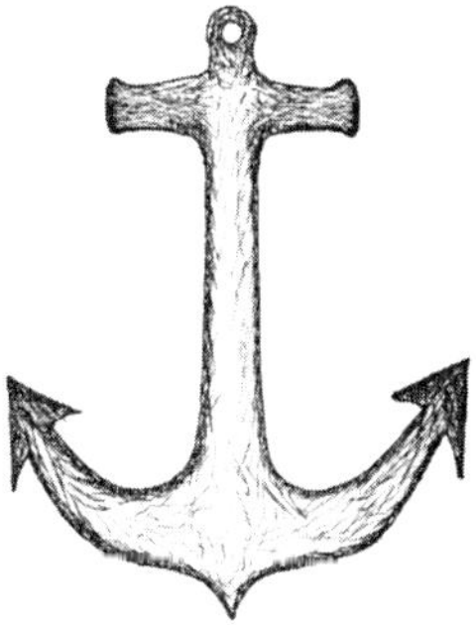

Give thanks to the Lord, call on his name . . . Sing praise to him . . . Let the hearts of those who seek the Lord rejoice. Look to the Lord and his strength; seek his face always.

from Psalm 105:1-4

I will say of the Lord, "He is my refuge and my fortress, my God, in whom I trust." He will cover you with his feathers, and under his wings you will find refuge; his faithfulness will be your shield and rampart. You will not fear the terror of night, nor the arrow that flies by day, nor the pestilence that stalks in the darkness, nor the plague that destroys at midday.

Psalm 91:2, 4-6

The name of the Lord is a fortified tower; the righteous run to it and are safe.

Proverbs 18:10

Get rid of all bitterness, rage and anger, brawling and slander, along with every form of malice. Be kind and compassionate to one another, forgiving each other, just as in Christ God forgave you.

Ephesians 4:31, 32

Let us then approach God's throne of grace with confidence, so that we may receive mercy and find grace to help us in our time of need.

Hebrews 4:16

He said to me, "My grace is sufficient for you, for my power is made perfect in weakness." Therefore I will boast all the more gladly about my weaknesses, so that Christ's power may rest on me. That is why, for Christ's sake, I delight in weaknesses, in insults, in hardships, in persecutions, in difficulties. For when I am weak, then I am strong.

2 Corinthians 12:9, 10

Rejoice in the Lord always. I will say it again: Rejoice! Let your gentleness be evident to all. The Lord is near.

Philippians 4:4, 5

Jewels' Reflections

Email to Carolee - first time through Section One

Tonight a little after 10 pm I went downstairs and focused on Section One, especially Hebrews 4:16. But when I got to Ephesians 4:31 and 32 the Holy Spirit brought someone from work to mind, so I stopped and prayed. Between Ephesians and Hebrews I became overwhelmed and started to cry. I asked God what was wrong with me. I couldn't stop crying, but through it I told the Lord that I loved him and trusted him even though I was in pain. *J*

Email - another time through Section One

Before I began, I confessed to God that I was struggling but I was also choosing to submit my anger, as well as the time, to him. I prayed and read Section One – slowly. I struggled with Ephesians 4:31 and 32, but Hebrews 4:16 saved the day. Later my mind was still trying to push past the anger. Out loud I said, "Lord I thank you for your peace because 'no weapon formed against me shall prosper'." I can happily report I am not angry. I am in it to win! *J*

Run to Me!

from Our Daily Bread

During a walk at a local park, my children and I encountered a couple of unleashed dogs. Their owner didn't seem to notice that one of them had begun to intimidate my son. My son tried to shoo the dog away, but the animal only became more intent on bothering him.

Eventually, my son panicked. He bolted several yards into the distance, but the dog pursued him. The chase continued until I yelled, "Run to me!" My son doubled back, calmed down and the dog finally decided to make mischief somewhere else.

There are moments in our lives when God calls to us and says, "Run to Me!" Something troubling is on our heels. The faster and farther we go, the more closely it pursues us. We can't shake it. We're too afraid to turn and confront the trouble on our own. But the reality is that we aren't on our own. God is there, ready to help and comfort us. All we have to do is turn away from whatever scares us, and move in his direction. His Word says in Proverbs 18:10, "The name of the Lord is a fortified tower; the righteous run to it and are safe." [10]

Section Two

GOD IS MY COMFORT

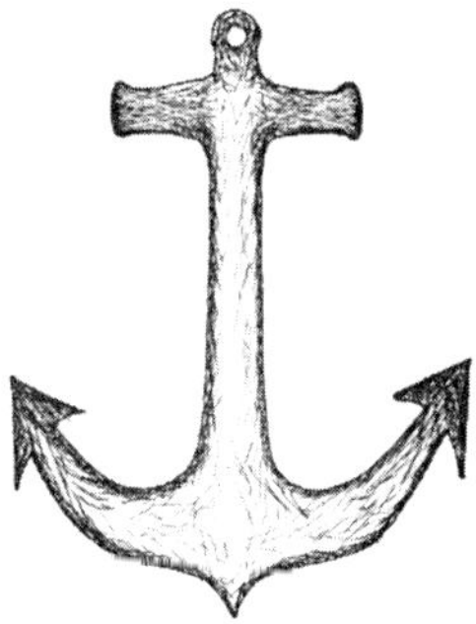

I will give thanks to You, Lord, with all my heart; I will tell of all your wonderful deeds. I will be glad and rejoice in You.

Psalm 9:1, 2

Your Word is a lamp to my feet and a light to my path.

Psalm 119:105

Even though I walk through the valley of the shadow of death, I will fear no evil, for You are with me; your rod and your staff, they comfort me.

Psalm 23:4

God is our refuge and strength, an ever-present help in trouble. Therefore we will not fear, though the earth give way and the mountains fall into the heart of the sea, though its waters roar and foam and the mountains quake with their surging.

Psalm 46:1-3

Be still, and know that I am God.

Psalm 46:10

I am the Lord your God who takes hold of your right hand and says to you, "Do not fear; I will help you."

Isaiah 41:13

Come to me, all you who are weary and burdened and I will give you rest. Take my yoke upon you and learn from me, for I am gentle and humble in heart and you will find rest for your souls. For my yoke is easy and my burden is light.

Matthew 11:28-30

I sought the Lord, and He heard me, and delivered me from all my fears.

Psalm 34:4

We know that in all things God works for the good of those who love him, who have been called according to his purpose.

Romans 8:28

Cast all your anxiety on him because He cares for you. Be self-controlled and alert. Your enemy the devil prowls around like a roaring lion looking for someone to devour. Resist him, standing firm in the faith.

1 Peter 5:7, 8

Thanks be to God! He gives us the victory through our Lord Jesus Christ.

1 Corinthians 15:57

Jewels' Reflections

Email to Carolee - first time through Section Two

So, today is my birthday. I talked to the Lord about today and what it meant to me, and then I dug into Section Two. A verse that stood out loudly was Psalm 119:105. When I read Psalm 46:1-3 I kept saying, "God is my refuge and my strength and my ever-present help when...." Each time I filled in the blank with something (when I'm angry, when I need wisdom, when I need to make a decision, etc.). Then I prayed and I didn't pay attention to the time because I just wanted to give God the time, however much it was. *J*

Emails - later times through Section Two

This evening I focused on Section Two again with extra attention to Psalm 119:105. God's Word brings illumination. When I got to the end I prayed, but also went back to each scripture and used "thank you" and "I will" where it was appropriate, kinda like a conversation. *J*

Hi Carolee, I read Section Two at my desk this afternoon, slowly. I kept reading the verses over and over slowly. I hung onto Psalm 46, that God is my refuge. *J*

Good evening. Thank you so very much for the time we spent on the phone today. I really felt like my head was going to explode. I was so overwhelmed! Many things you said today brought me comfort.

Tonight I focused on Section Two. I felt like the Holy Spirit was speaking Psalm 119:105 to me. At the end I thanked God for his Word being my lamp and light, and it's like He said, "as long as you walk in my Word you won't be in the dark." Meaning that my thoughts and feelings won't drag me to the edge of a cliff all the time. I'm really encouraged with that! *J*

Perspectives on Anxiety

Dr. Caroline Leaf in *Switch on Your Brain*

An undisciplined mind is filled with a continuous stream of worries, fears and distorted perceptions that trigger degenerative processes in the mind and body. We cannot afford not to bring all our thoughts into captivity to Jesus Christ. [11]

Research dating back to the 1970s shows that capturing our thoughts in a disciplined way rather than letting them run chaotically can bring about impressive changes in how we feel and think.... My research shows that controlled focused thinking leads to improvements in cognitive functioning and emotional balance. [12]

If you change your attitude and determine to apply God's excellent advice not to worry, the hypothalamus will cause the secretion of chemicals that facilitate the feeling of peace, and the rest of the brain will respond by secreting the correct formula of neurotransmitters . . . for thought-building and clear thinking. [13]

Section Three

GOD IS MY PROTECTOR

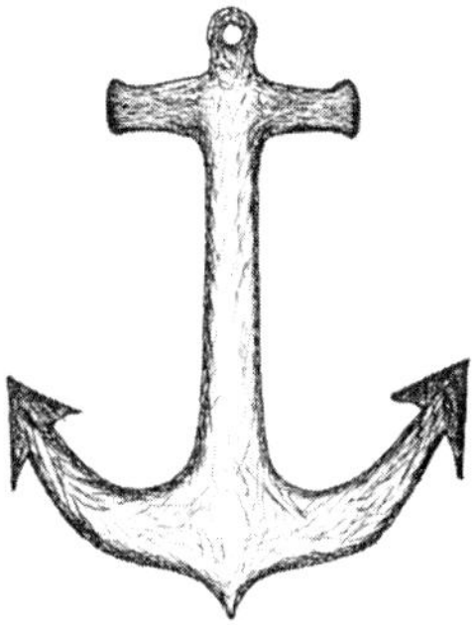

The Lord lives! Praise be to my Rock!
Exalted be God my Saviour!

Psalm 18:46

I trust in God, so why should I be afraid?
What can mere mortals do to me?

Psalm 56:11 NLT

If we are thrown into the blazing furnace, the God we serve is able to deliver us from it, and He will deliver us from Your Majesty's hand. But even if He does not, we want you to know, Your Majesty, that we will not serve your gods or worship the image of gold you have set up.

Daniel 3:17, 18 NIVUK

Our protection is from the Lord himself.

Psalm 89:18 TLB

Do not be anxious about anything, but in every situation, by prayer and petition, with thanksgiving, present your requests to God. And the peace of God, which transcends all understanding, will guard your hearts and your minds in Christ Jesus.

Philippians 4:6, 7

When I am afraid, I put my trust in You.

Psalm 56:3

I will both lay me down in peace and sleep, for Thou Lord only makest me dwell in safety.

Psalm 4:8 KJV

You will keep in perfect peace all who trust in You, all whose thoughts are fixed on You.

Isaiah 26:3

You are my refuge and my shield; I have put my hope in your Word.

Psalm 119:114

Be joyful always, pray continually, give thanks in all circumstances, for this is God's will for you in Christ Jesus.

1 Thessalonians 5:16-18

God has not given us a spirit of fear, but of power and of love and of a sound mind.

2 Timothy 1:7 NKJV

Submit to God. Resist the devil and he will flee from you. Draw near to God and He will draw near to you.

James 4:7, 8 NKJV

The temptations in your life are no different from what others experience. And God is faithful. He will not allow the temptation to be more than you can stand. When you are tempted, He will show you a way out so that you can endure.

1 Corinthians 10:13 NLT

Jewels' Reflections

Email to Carolee - after first time through Section Three

Good morning Carolee, I didn't get a chance to call you yesterday after I was finished. I fought my brain and spent about 30 minutes in my room yesterday, candle lit, Anchor Verses in hand. I focused on Section Three. The verses that really stood out to me were Psalm 56:3 and 1 Thessalonians 5:16-18, and of course James 4:7-8. My mind fought me even though I did submit, resist, draw near. I could never thank you enough for your patience and your kindness. *J*

Email - another time through Section Three

Tonight I focused on Section Three. When I got to Psalm 56:3 I felt sad. I stopped, and started confessing some pretty significant fears that I have. I confessed each one and asked for forgiveness, then spoke Psalm 56:3. I found great comfort in Psalm 4:8. I sat quietly for a few minutes, then asked God to bring the scriptures to mind all day long. *J*

You are my strength,
I watch for You;
You, God, are my fortress,
my God on whom I can rely . . .

I will sing of your strength,
In the morning
I will sing of your love;
For You are my fortress,
my refuge in times of trouble.

You are my strength,
I sing praise to You;
You, God, are my fortress,
my God on whom I can rely.
From Psalm 59:9, 10, 16, 17

How Fear Affects Us

Dr. Neil T. Anderson in *The Bondage Breaker*

Fear weakens us,
causes us to be self-centered
and clouds our minds
so that all we can think about
is the thing that frightens us.
But fear can only control us if we let it. [14]

Section Four

GOD IS MY STRENGTH

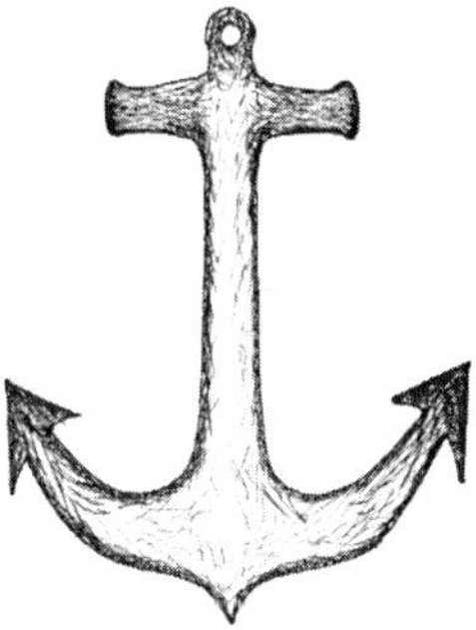

O God, You are my God! Your love and kindness are better to me than life itself. How I praise You! I will bless You as long as I live, lifting up my hands to You in prayer.

Psalm 63:1, 3, 4

To You, O Lord, I lift up my soul; in You I trust, O my God.

Psalm 25:1

The Lord is my light and my salvation - so why should I be afraid? The Lord is my fortress, protecting me from danger, so why should I tremble?

Psalm 27:1

This is what the Lord says, He who created you . . . He who formed you . . . "Fear not, for I have redeemed you; I have [called] you by name, you are mine. When you pass through the waters, I will be with you; and when you pass through the rivers, they will not [overwhelm] you; when you walk through the fire you will not be burned, the flames will not set you ablaze. For I am the Lord, your God, the Holy One . . . your Saviour . . . You are precious and honoured in my sight . . . I love you . . . Do not be afraid, for I am with you."

from Isaiah 43:1-5
adapted

When anxiety was great within me, your consolation brought me joy.

Psalm 94:19

Have I not commanded you? Be strong and courageous. Do not be afraid; do not be discouraged, for the Lord your God will be with you wherever you go.

Joshua 1:9

We have this treasure in jars of clay to show that this all-surpassing power is from God and not from us. We are hard pressed on every side, but not crushed; perplexed, but not in despair; persecuted, but not abandoned; struck down, but not destroyed.

2 Corinthians 4:7-9

I can do all things through Christ who strengthens me.

Philippians 4:13 NKJV

Being confident of this, that He who began a good work in you will carry it on to completion until the day of Christ Jesus.

Philippians 1:6

Thanks be to God who always leads us in triumphal procession in Christ and through us spreads everywhere the fragrance of the knowledge of him.

2 Corinthians 2:14

Jewels' Reflections

Email to Carolee - after first time through Section Four

This evening I focused on Section Four, making sure to use thankfulness before each part of each scripture. I stopped halfway and asked the Holy Spirit to fill every corner of our house with his peace and to just be with me.

I made the scriptures personal to me, for example, for Psalm 94:19 I said, "Your Word says 'be anxious for nothing,' but when my flesh chooses anxiety, and I am overwhelmed, I thank you that your consolation will bring me joy." Today Joshua 1:9 held special meaning for me. And 2 Corinthians 4:8 and 9. Section Four is packed with so much good stuff!

As I was staring at the stillness of the flame of the candle I felt like He said, "Be still like the flame." So I began to say, "You are my light when I am pressured, You are my light when I am perplexed, You are my light when I am persecuted, You are my light when I am struck down." And what a great way to finish with Philippians 1:6. *J*

Email - another time through Section Four

I went downstairs this evening and decided to focus on Section Four again. I pored over the scriptures slowly, and could hardly get past Isaiah 43. God is with me no matter what! I belong to him no matter what! With each scripture I thanked him for his Word and his presence. I so love Section Four! *J*

God says -

I care about you. Matthew 10:31

I am with you. Joshua 1:9

I will provide for you. Philippians 4:19

I will deliver you. Psalm 72:12

I have a purpose for you. 2 Corinthians 4:7

Trusting God's Promises

"Standing on the Promises" was written in 1886 by Russell Kelso Carter. Carter's career included being a star athlete, a teacher, a coach, a Methodist minister and last of all, a medical doctor. He understood what it was to trust God's promises instead of giving in to fear.

At the age of 30 he was diagnosed with a serious heart condition for which there was no treatment at the time. Carter prayerfully put his trust in God. That experience led him to writing "Standing on the Promises," which became the most popular of the many songs he wrote. He lived to the age of 78 years.[15]

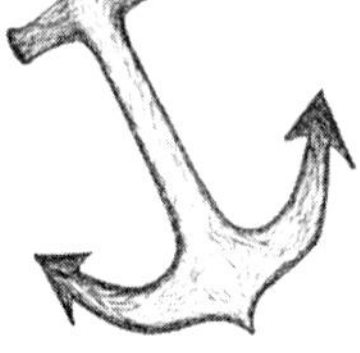

Standing on the Promises

Standing on the promises
of Christ my King,
Through eternal ages let his praises ring.
Glory in the highest,
I will shout and sing,
Standing on the promises of God.

Standing on the promises
that cannot fail,
When the howling storms of doubt
and fear assail.
By the living Word of God
I shall prevail.
Standing on the promises of God.

Russel Kelso Carter, 1886

My child, pay attention to what I say.
  Listen carefully to my words.
    Don't lose sight of them.
Let them penetrate deep into your heart,
  for they bring life to those who find them,
    and healing to their whole body.

Proverbs 4:20-22 NLT

Section Five

GOD IS MY PROVIDER

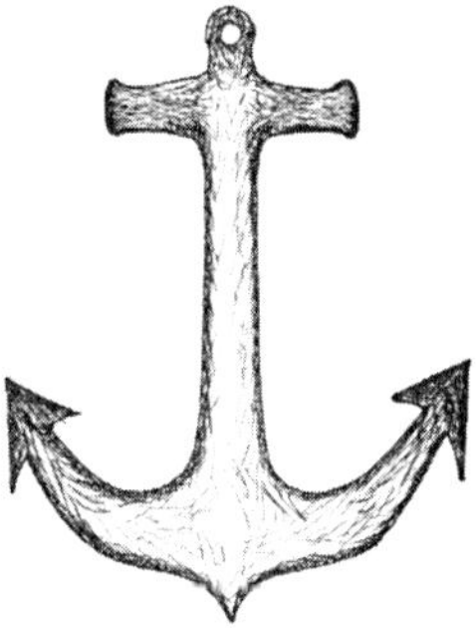

Praise the Lord, O my soul, all my inmost being, praise his holy name. Praise the Lord, O my soul and forget not all his benefits.

Psalm 103:1, 2

Search me, O God, and know my heart; test me and know my anxious thoughts.

Psalm 139:23

So do not fear, for I am with you; do not be dismayed, for I am your God. I will strengthen you and help you; I will uphold you with my righteous right hand.

Isaiah 41:10

[Jesus said] Therefore I tell you, do not worry about your life, what you will eat or drink; or about your body, what you will wear. Is not life more important than food, and the body more important than clothes? Look at the birds of the air; they do not sow or reap or store away in barns, and yet your heavenly Father feeds them. Are you not much more valuable than they? Who of you by worrying can add a single hour to your life? And why do you worry about clothes? See how the lilies of the field grow. They do not labour or spin. Yet I tell you that not even Solomon in all his splendour was dressed like one of these.

If that is how God clothes the grass of the field, which is here today and tomorrow is thrown into the fire, will He not much more clothe you, O you of little faith? So do not worry, saying, 'What shall we eat?' or 'What shall we drink?' or 'What shall we wear?' For the pagans run after all these things, and your heavenly Father knows that you need them. But seek first his kingdom and his righteousness, and all these things will be given to you as well. Therefore do not worry about tomorrow, for tomorrow will worry about itself. Each day has enough trouble of its own.

Matthew 6:25-34

My God will meet all your needs according to the riches of his glory in Christ Jesus.

Philippians 4:19

Keep your eyes fixed on Jesus.

Hebrews 12:2

Cast your burden on the Lord, and He will sustain you.

Psalm 55:22

Now may the Lord of peace himself give you peace at all times in every way.

2 Thessalonians 3:16

Jewels' Reflections

Email to Carolee - first time through Section Five

Ohhhhh I almost didn't! I'm feeling under the weather and my mind kept saying, "Just lie on the couch. You feel terrible, so it's okay." But the moment I put my son to bed I grabbed the candle and headed downstairs. I focused on Section Five, which is filled with some of my favourite scriptures! I held onto Isaiah 41:10 (of course) and I really digested Matthew 6:25-34. With Philippians 4:19 coming right after, it was like a double-shot of, "Stop worrying!" The needs for me are: peace, trusting in God, resting in him, and giving my thought life over to his Word. I prayed and I think it was maybe 15 or 20 minutes I was there. When bed time came, I couldn't sleep, and I lay there thinking about Jesus, and whispering to him and the room was filled with peace… Then the alarm went off!! Please continue to pray for me to NOT stop asking, seeking and knocking. *J*

Email - another time through Section Five

Good evening Carolee, I hope you had an enjoyable day. Today my time was spent in Section Five. I spoke each scripture slowly, thinking about how each one is changing my mind and ultimately my brain and also picturing God saying them to me. I really thought long and hard about Psalm 139:23, especially, "Try me and know my anxieties." The nine verses in Matthew were also extra comforting tonight. And I will tell myself Hebrews 12:2 all the time. The more I read, the more the scriptures are sticking. *J*

I will study your commandments
and reflect on your ways.
I will delight in your decrees
and not forget your Word.
Psalm 119:15, 16 NLT

Always

Always I am with you,
All night long I'm here.
Do not trust your feelings,
Don't give in to fear.
Remember what I said to you,
That I will never leave;
I will not forsake you,
My word you must believe.

Always I am with you,
All day long I will be there.
I'm watching as you come and go,
Your ev'ry moment I long to share.
Don't forget – it's I who made you
And all your days I've planned.
I will give you strength,
And uphold you with my hand.

Always I am with you.
Always I will be
Behind you and before you;
Put your trust in Me.
Of this you can be confident,
Of this you can be sure:
Though war break out against you
You who fear Me shall endure.

Always I am with you
Always I am near.
Call to Me – I'll answer,
Because you love Me I will hear.
There is nothing man can do to you,
For I hide you 'neath my wings.
With my feathers I will cover you,
Full of joy, your heart will sing.

Always I am with you, Always. [16]

Connie Smith, 2000

The Robin and the Sparrow

Said the Robin to the Sparrow
"I would surely like to know
Why these anxious human beings
Rush about and worry so."

Said the Sparrow to the Robin,
"Friend, I think that it must be
They have no Heavenly Father
Such as cares for you and me." [17]

Elizabeth Cheney, 1859

Section Six

GOD IS MY SOURCE

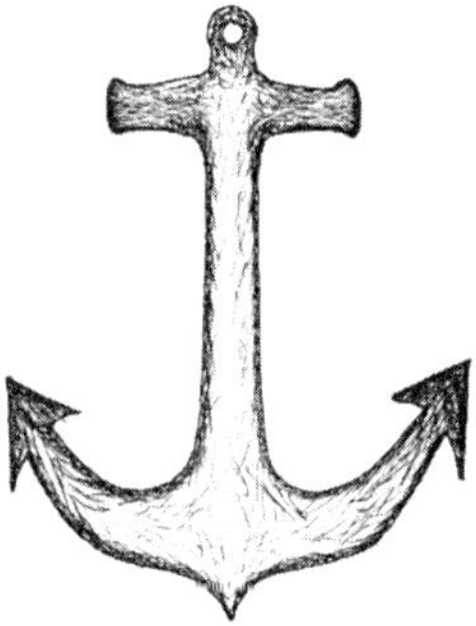

My soul finds rest in God; my salvation comes from him. He alone is my rock and my salvation; He is my fortress, I will never be shaken.

Psalm 62:1, 2

Be still before the Lord and wait patiently for him; do not fret - it leads only to evil.

Psalm 37:7a, 8b

Jesus said, "If you hold to my teaching, you are really my disciples. Then you will know the truth, and the truth will set you free."

John 8:31, 32

Therefore, as God's chosen people, holy and dearly loved, clothe yourselves with compassion, kindness, humility, gentleness and patience. Bear with each other and forgive whatever grievances you may have against one another. Forgive as the Lord forgave you.

Colossians 3:12, 13

Trust in the Lord with all your heart, and do not lean on your own understanding. In all your ways acknowledge him, and He will make your paths straight.

Proverbs 3:5, 6

The Lord himself goes before you and will be with you; He will never leave you nor forsake you. Do not be afraid; do not be discouraged.

Deuteronomy 31:8

Though we live in the world, we do not wage war as the world does. The weapons we fight with are not the weapons of the world. On the contrary, they have divine power to demolish strongholds. We demolish arguments and every pretension that sets itself up against the knowledge of God, and we take captive every thought to make it obedient to Christ.

2 Corinthians 10:3-5

So we can say boldly, "The Lord helps me. I will not be afraid. What can mere human beings do to me?" Jesus Christ is the same yesterday and today and forever.

Hebrews 13:6, 8 NIrV

Finally, brothers and sisters, whatever is true, whatever is noble, whatever is right, whatever is pure, whatever is lovely, whatever is admirable - if anything is excellent or praiseworthy - think about such things.

Philippians 4:8

Jewels' Reflections

Email to Carolee - first time through Section Six
Today I focused on Section Six. One of the verses that stood out was Deuteronomy 31:8. I kept saying: "The Lord goes before me AND He is with me; He never leaves me, He never forsakes me. I will not be afraid, I will not be discouraged." I said it slowly and repeatedly. I also kept saying Philippians 4:8, "I will not be discouraged if I think on things that are true, noble, right, pure, lovely, admirable, excellent and praiseworthy." *J*

Email - another time through Section Six
Good evening Carolee, I hope you had a good weekend. I spent time in my room yesterday morning and focused on Section Six. I then memorized Psalm 62:1 and 2 and carried them with me all day. Deuteronomy 31:8 also brought me comfort. "He goes before me and He is with me!" 2 Corinthians 10:3-5 is always a great reminder for me. The day was really good!

Jewels

Anchor Verses

By now you may have discovered that this is not a "self-help" book. It is a guide for reaching out to the Lord in trust and gratitude. In doing so you will experience the "peace of God, which transcends all understanding." It will guard your heart and your mind (Philippians 4:6, 7).

As you continue using the Anchor Verses to overcome worry, fear and anxiety, you may want to have them conveniently tucked in with your Bible and journal.

With that in mind, the Anchor Verses are available as a PDF in two formats so that you can print them and keep them at hand or give them to a friend. The End Notes include a link to the Living Free blog. When the page opens, the two formats are listed at the top. Choose the one you want and the document will appear on your screen and you can print it. [18]

Change the Channel to Worship

Do you remember that each of the six sections of Anchor Verses started with praise and worship?

When we are full of worry and fear we tend to focus on ourselves, our problems and our feelings. When we worship God we get our eyes off ourselves. Instead of being preoccupied with our distressing circumstances and our bad feelings, we turn our eyes to the One who is powerful, loving and caring. It's like changing channels on the television.

Worship can be as simple as directing your thoughts to what you appreciate about God. It can be as simple as telling God you love him! It could be reading a psalm of joy or listening to praise music.

Each day and each anxiety is an opportunity to change the channel in your brain and focus on your amazing God. Worship will overcome your fears and anxieties.

Turn your eyes upon Jesus,
Look full in his wonderful face,
And the things of earth will grow strangely dim,
In the light of his glory and grace. [19]

Helen H Lemmel, 1918

Praise the Lord, my soul;
  all my inmost being, praise his holy name.

Praise the Lord, my soul,
  and forget not all his benefits.
The Lord is compassionate and gracious,
  slow to anger, abounding in love.
He will not always accuse,
  nor will He harbour his anger forever;
He does not treat us as our sins deserve
  or repay us according to our iniquities.
For as high as the heavens are above the earth,
  so great is his love for those who fear him;
as far as the east is from the west,
  so far has He removed our transgressions from us.
As a father has compassion on his children,
  so the Lord has compassion on those who fear him.

Psalm 103:1, 2, 8-13

Added Value

You have been absorbing verses of comfort and encouragement rather than dwelling on anxious thoughts. Are you ready to enlarge and enrich your daily routine? If not, simply continue using the Anchor Verses. If yes, the next few pages will show how you can benefit even more as you use these Bible verses.

No need to try all the ideas at once. You could aim to incorporate them over a period of several weeks. You can add them in any order.

What if you don't succeed? *Don't get stressed about it!* Just continue to renew your mind in the Word. As you gain more peace, you may be ready to include some of the useful strategies in the following pages.

May the word of God dwell richly
In my heart from hour to hour,
So that all may see I triumph
Only through his power. [20]

Kate B. Wilkinson, 1925

Starting Well

2 minutes

It is helpful to prepare yourself physically, mentally and spiritually each day before using the Anchor Verses. Here are some ways to do that.

- Choose a quiet comfortable *location*. Sit with good *posture*.
- Offer brief *thanksgiving* and *praise* to God. You may wish to light a candle and thank God that Jesus is the light of the world and the light of your life.
- *Notice* what is around you, the sights and sounds. Then *notice* your thoughts. Are there worries or stresses? If so, picture yourself before the cross of Christ with a bundle of burdens. Then picture yourself putting those burdens down at the cross and leaving them there. Jesus is your burden-bearer.
- Take a few long, slow, deep *breaths* and relax your body.
- *Prayerfully* place your mind and heart in God's care.

Reflecting

2 minutes

Reflection has a powerful, positive impact on the brain. According to Dr. Caroline Leaf, intentional reflection is an important tool for developing new healthy pathways of thought in the brain.[21] Here is one way to be thoughtful in a productive way.

Recall briefly a way that worry and anxiety has affected your life. You may think of the past hour or the past day. Or you may wish to choose something from the past week or year. It will have more benefit if you write down your recollection in a sentence or two. (See next page.)

Focus briefly on a change you want to see in your life. Imagine one way it would be different if you were free of anxiety. Take a moment to put this down on paper. (See next page.)

You may want to draw or doodle instead of using words to record your reflections.

Writing

3 minutes

Writing your reflections is helpful in overcoming fear and anxiety.

Maybe you don't like writing so you are about to skip this page. Before you do, keep in mind that writing down your thoughts helps you to clarify what is on your mind. It helps to establish the new patterns that you want to embed in your brain. If you take time to write your reflections on fear and anxiety or on any toxic thinking, it will contribute to the changes you are hoping for.

Here's how to do it simply

- Each day put down the date in your notebook.
- *Write* your reflections briefly. (See previous page.)
- *Reread* thoughtfully; feel free to make changes.

Here are other ways to "notch it up"

- Write down anything you sense God saying to you.
- Write your thanks to God for any progress you see in becoming more peaceful, less anxious.

Reading the Anchor Verses

3 minutes

The Anchor Verses are the core of this book. Receiving God's encouraging Word into your heart and mind will bring you peace and confidence and will enhance any other strategy that you are using to overcome anxiety.

If you are able to read in the morning, you have the benefit of the truths being fresh on your mind as the day unfolds. If you read in the evening, plan to carry the truths into the next day.

Remember the instructions given earlier

- Read the verses *slowly* out loud. Skip over the references for a better flow in reading.
- Read *thoughtfully*.
- Receive the truths as God's gift for you today.

After you have read the verses glance back over them and thank God for specific truths you noticed. Accept them as words of encouragement and comfort that God is giving you. They are your anchors.

Write down truths that you thank God for. (2 minutes)

Taking a Truth into Your Day

3 minutes

Choose a verse for the day. (1 minute) If you are already doing this, great! If not, this is the time to add it to your daily practice! Remember, don't agonize about choosing a verse. Any Anchor Verse is fine. Record the reference in your journal.

Prepare the verse, either by writing it out, which is good for the brain, or by using the computer to print copies to put in various places. (2 minutes)

Place the verse where you will see it often.

Repeat the verse out loud *at least seven times during the day* as you notice it. Each time receive it as a gift from God. Imagine holding it to your heart – embracing it. If you want to notch it up, memorize the verse.

What your mouth speaks and your ears hear increases the impact on your mind. Your goal is to switch from anxious thoughts to thoughts of trusting in Christ. It takes repetition to "be transformed by the renewing of your mind" (Romans 12:2).

Bringing it All Together

Now that you have seen the various aspects of Added Value, here is a summary of how you can bring it together to use over a period of weeks. [22]

- *Start well:* Settle yourself in a quiet spot. Notice what is on your mind, take a deep breath and shift to thanksgiving, praise and worship. Then request God's help and strength. (2 minutes)
- *Reflect:* Remind yourself of one fear that bothers you and consider its impact on your life. (1 minute) Focus on some aspect of this process, e.g. the outcomes you hope for, your progress, new insights the Holy Spirit is showing you. (1 minute)
- *Write* down briefly what you have just been thinking about. (2 minutes)
- *Reread* what you wrote. Change it if you are inclined or if the Spirit prompts you. (1 minute)
- *Read* aloud the Anchor Verse section for the day - slowly, thoughtfully and thankfully. (3 minutes)
- *Write* down a few thoughts on what these verses mean to you. (2 minutes)

- *Choose a biblical truth:* Pick a verse for the day. Write the reference in your notebook. (1 minute)
- *Renew your mind:* Write out the verse you picked or make multiple copies. (2 minutes) Put the verse in strategic places so that you will see it throughout the day. Plan to pause and *read it at least 7 times through the day.*
- Keep going for 3 weeks! Why so many times a day for so long? Because scientists say it takes that to change a thought pathway in the brain.
- Remember the advice to find someone who will encourage you on this journey. (See page 32.)

Stronghold Busting is a similar approach. It adds a declaration that you prepare: "I renounce the lie that… I announce the truth that…." Please see the endnotes for further information. [23]

Good reminders from Dr. Caroline Leaf

You cannot sit back and wait to be happy and healthy and have a great thought life; you have to make the choice to make this happen. [24]

We need to be almost obsessive in our desire to change. [25]

Helpful Strategies

for overcoming worry, anxiety and fear

Check these out and choose a few to start with, then add more

Be physical; it improves the emotional

- go for walks; exercise regularly
- eat healthy foods
- reduce caffeine and sugar (increase protein to reduce sugar craving)
- get enough rest

Pay attention to the mental and emotional

- replace negative thoughts with thoughts that are comforting, encouraging and hopeful
- forget about trying to be perfect
- drop the "shoulds" for self and other people
- don't "awfulize" or "catastrophize"
- accept that there are some days that are harder than others; that's life!

Make sure you have supports

- see a physician and a counsellor
- join a group - Bible Study or Care Group
- get help to stop depending on substances

Relationships are important

- keep connected to healthy people and Christian people; don't isolate
- do something nice for someone each day

Refreshing things to do

- have a Quiet Time, if possible early in the day - read the Bible thoughtfully and pray
- journal, if that is enjoyable
- read good books or articles
- make time for a hobby or sport that you enjoy
- limit TV and media; limit fear-raising information
- take time for things that bring laughter

When you start feeling stressed, follow a simple plan that you have memorized. For example -

- *refresh* - pause and take a slow, deep breath, then let it out slowly
- *recall* an encouraging Bible verse or good quote
- *refocus* - go for a walk, sing, work, read or call someone - basically, do something!

The Benefits Are Tremendous

by John Neufeld, pastor of The Meeting Place in Winnipeg

This past weekend I again discovered how anxiety had crept into my life and was having a negative impact on me. The crazy thing is, I wasn't truly aware of the negative effect of anxiety on me until it was gone. Here is the story in a nutshell.

We own a small cabin that is sitting on sandy clay soil and the foundation was shifting, causing cracks in the building. This bothered me, but foundation work is physically difficult and expensive. I was avoiding the work because of both the expense and the challenge of the job. Well this past Saturday, I got the job done. Gratefully it was less expensive than anticipated, and this morning my body is sore, because it was every bit as physically challenging as I expected.

After the work was done, I quickly became aware of how quiet my mind was. The mental and emotional background noise that anxiety created was consuming more energy and attention than I realized.

This noise was affecting my relationship with my family, it was affecting my work, and it was affecting my relationship with Jesus.

Take a moment and read these words of scripture.

Philippians 4:6, 7 Do not be anxious about anything, but in every situation, by prayer and petition, with thanksgiving, present your requests to God. And the peace of God, which transcends all understanding, will guard your hearts and your minds in Christ Jesus.

1 Peter 5:5-9 In the same way, you who are younger, submit yourselves to your elders. All of you, clothe yourselves with humility toward one another, because "God opposes the proud but shows favour to the humble." Humble yourselves, therefore, under God's mighty hand, that He may lift you up in due time. Cast all your anxiety on him because He cares for you. Be alert and of sober mind. Your enemy the devil prowls around like a roaring lion looking for someone to devour. Resist him, standing firm in the faith, because you know that the family of believers throughout the world is undergoing the same kind of sufferings.

cont'd ⇨

(Benefits cont'd)

Psalm 139:23, 24 Search me, God, and know my heart; test me and know my anxious thoughts. See if there is any offensive way in me, and lead me in the way everlasting.

After reading these Bible verses a couple of things occur to me.

- There are practical concerns in life that when unaddressed have a harmful effect on us and on our relationships. *SOLVE THEM.* The anxiety and its effect is worse than the cost of addressing the problem. As followers of Jesus, filled with the Holy Spirit, we can trust God to take us through these challenges. So pay off your credit cards, answer that email you have been avoiding, pick up the phone and call _________, fix the dripping faucet. You get the idea.
- There are anxieties caused by our own insecurities, our need for recognition, and our self-importance. *CONFESS THEM.* Confession is one of the great ways we cast our cares on God. The book of James [5:16] tells us to "confess your sins to each other and pray for each other so that you may be healed. The prayer of a righteous person is

powerful and effective." Confession heals us from a lot of anxiety.

- There are circumstances where others are conspiring against us. These are real relational and spiritual battles. *TRUST GOD.* I mean it. Outline in detail the circumstances in prayer. Be thorough about it. Ask the Holy Spirit to give you great wisdom and courage to act rightly. Things may not resolve favourably, but we do not need to be anxious, because God is with us in the midst of the battle.

In the past couple of days I have thought new thoughts because the anxiety was gone, I have been a more attentive dad and husband because the anxiety was gone, I have slept better because the anxiety was gone. So, what's next on the list? I want to deal with it because *the benefits are tremendous.* [26]

John Neufeld

Knowing Jesus, the Living Word

Knowing Jesus personally is the most important way of overcoming fear.

If you have never given your life to Christ, here is an opportunity. Admit that you need him as your Saviour. Ask Jesus to forgive your sins and change you. Make a commitment to live for him instead of for yourself.

When you do that, many things happen.

- You become a child of God.
- You are a new person in Christ.
- You receive the gift of eternal life.
- The Holy Spirit comes into your life and He helps you to overcome worry, fear and anxiety.

> For God so loved the world that He gave his one and only Son, that whoever believes in him shall not perish but have eternal life. John 3:16

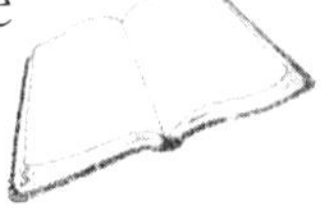

Becoming a Child of God

Would you like Jesus to be your Saviour? Here is a suggested prayer for becoming a child of God. First read it carefully and if you have questions, ask a pastor or a friend who is a Christian.

Lord Jesus, I need You. Today I call upon You for my salvation. I confess that I have sinned. I believe in my heart that You died on the cross for my sins. Please forgive me and cleanse my life. Thank you for being my Saviour and making me part of your family. I believe that You were raised from the dead and because of that I can have eternal life with You. I choose to be your follower and I commit myself to You, as Lord of my life. Amen

After you have prayed, thank God in your own words for giving you the gift of forgiveness and the gift of eternal life. You are now his child! People experience this new life in different ways. If your emotions fluctuate, trust God to hold you close. He will!

To the New Follower of Christ

a word from Ken

Hi,

Are you a new believer in Jesus? If so, He has given you his life! You become new when you ask Jesus to forgive your sins.

God has done a whole series of incredible things for you and you can rest in his love and care for you. It is only natural to respond to him with loving him back and expressing your thankfulness.

Let him know how you feel and ask him how He feels, especially about you. He is thrilled that you are in his family. Check out Zephaniah 3:17 on page 11 and Isaiah 43:1-5 on page 57. Reading the Bible will help you to find out more about God and about yourself!

As you connect with his people (hint: many of them go to church) you will experience joy and encouragement. Ask about being baptized because Jesus would be pleased if you took that step to make your commitment known to others.

Some things may be hard but God is with you. The Holy Spirit will comfort you. He will strengthen and guide you.

Congratulations on becoming a Christ-follower and welcome to the family!

Ken

P.S. Here are affirming words from the first letter of John.

If we confess our sins, He is faithful and just and will forgive us our sins and purify us from all unrighteousness. 1 John 1:9

See what great love the Father has lavished on us, that we should be called children of God! And that is what we are! 1 John 3:1

And so we know and rely on the love God has for us. God is love. Whoever lives in love lives in God, and God in them. There is no fear in love. But perfect love drives out fear. 1 John 4:16 and 18a

What's Your Identity?

If someone asked you to describe yourself you would probably include what you do and where you live. You might talk about your interests and abilities such as music and sports or your hobbies and past times.

What about your identity as a Christian? Is it which church you attend or what you believe? Dr. Neil T. Anderson gets to the core of the matter. "I believe that your hope for growth, meaning and fulfilment as a Christian is based on understanding who you are - specifically your identity in Christ as a child of God." [27] He sums it up with Bible verses that have been fondly called the "Who I Am's." The partial list on the next page gives you a glimpse of your most important identity - being a child of God. [28]

Without understanding your spiritual identity, you will struggle and be prone to worry and defeat. The "Who I Am in Christ" list will give you a true perspective. Speak it out loud. Or use the statements to say thank you to God. Embrace the biblical truths with your whole being!

Who I am in Christ

I am no longer rejected, unloved, dirty or shameful.
In Christ I am completely accepted. God says:

I am God's child. John 1:12
I am Christ's friend. John 15:15
I am a saint, a holy one. Ephesians 1:1
I have been redeemed and forgiven of all my sins. Colossians 1:14

I am no longer guilty, unprotected, alone or abandoned.
In Christ I am totally secure. God says:

I am free from any condemning charges against me. Romans 8:31-34
I cannot be separated from the love of God. Romans 8:35-39
I am kept safe with Christ in God. Colossians 3:3
I can find grace and mercy to help in time of need. Hebrews 4:16
I am assured that all things work together for good. Romans 8:28
I have not been given a spirit of fear, but of power, love and a sound mind. 2 Timothy 1:7

I am no longer worthless, inadequate, helpless or hopeless.
In Christ I am deeply significant and special. God says:

I am a temple of God where the Holy Spirit lives. 1 Corinthians 3:16
I am chosen and appointed by God to bear fruit. John 15:16
I am God's workmanship, created for good works. Ephesians 2:10
I am a minister of reconciliation for God. 2 Corinthians 5:17-21
I may approach God with freedom and confidence. Ephesians 3:12
I can do all things through Christ who strengthens me! Philippians 4:13

My response: *I choose to receive the love of Christ and embrace these wonderful gifts He has for me.*

Doubts

Ken's story of anxiety

I committed my life to Christ when I was 11. It happened at a big event where I raised my hand and someone prayed with me. But afterwards I was confused. Was Jesus really in my life? I wasn't sure.

Most of the time in my teen and young adult years, I was a happy Christian, serving God. But some days I was distressed. At times I would break down and cry. Living with uncertainty was very painful and it caused me a lot of inner fear.

At the age of 29 I resolved this doubt when I prayed a prayer similar to what is on the opposite page. It was a memorable event for me. From then on I could say, "I know I am a child of God. It's a done deal!" The worries and doubts about salvation left me.

I am convinced that one of Satan's tricks is causing doubt! I am also convinced that God wants us to be assured. Confidence in being a Christian brings peace and joy. If you have doubts and fears, the way I did, I hope you will take a step of gaining assurance.

Prayer and Declaration about Doubts

Prayer for assurance of salvation

Lord Jesus, I affirm that I have called upon You for my salvation. I believe in my heart that You died on the cross for my sins and were raised from the dead so that I can have eternal life. I choose not to depend on feelings. I affirm that I am your follower. Thank you for making me your child. I now submit myself to You and invite You to be Lord of my life. Amen

Declaration against the enemy [29]

In the name of Jesus Christ, I renounce all the accusations of Satan that would rob me of my full assurance of eternal life. I have been transferred out of the kingdom of darkness and into God's kingdom of light. I declare that I am a child of God according to the assurance of John 1:12, "To all who received him, to those who believed in his name, He gave the right to become children of God." [30]

Following Jesus

singing in the dark

Following Jesus landed Paul and Silas in jail. Sitting in a dark, damp cell with torn and bloody backs, they began to sing. Acts 16:16-34 tells the fascinating story.

Songs of confidence in God bring light and hope into the darkness of fear and anxiety.

Do you like to sing? Then sing songs of praise to God. Sing songs of comfort and encouragement.

You don't sing? Then put on music. Listen to others singing the uplifting truths of scripture.

You don't have music accessible? Then hum or whisper the words of a spiritual song you appreciate. Music will encourage your mind and heart.

Great is Thy faithfulness!
Great is Thy faithfulness!
Morning by morning new mercies I see;
All I have needed Thy hand hath provided –
Great is Thy faithfulness, Lord, unto me!

Thomas Chisholm, 1923

Songs and Hymns

After they had been severely flogged, they were thrown into prison, and the jailer was commanded to guard them carefully. When he received these orders, he put them in the inner cell and fastened their feet in the stocks. About midnight Paul and Silas were praying and singing hymns to God, and the other prisoners were listening to them.

Acts 16:23-25

Sing psalms and hymns and spiritual songs to God with thankful hearts.

Colossians 3:16 NLT

Speak to one another with psalms, hymns and songs from the Spirit. Sing and make music from your heart to the Lord.

Ephesians 5:19 NIrV

Change Agent

Have you felt hopeless about overcoming worry, fear and anxiety? You have tried and tried and it only gets worse? Maybe you have gone from general anxiety to having panic attacks.

Don't despair, God has given the Holy Spirit to those who become his children through faith in Jesus Christ. That makes all the difference.

The Holy Spirit is called the Comforter, the Counsellor, the Helper, the Advocate, the Spirit of Truth and more. When you read the Bible the Holy Spirit is speaking to your heart. He is giving you hope and He is the one who brings you peace.

The Holy Spirit shows each of us where we need to change. That is called conviction. Then the Holy Spirit gives us strength to change. We need to quit trying in our own strength. This is crucial! You are supposed to be depending on the Holy Spirit, not on your own determination. Tell God you are weak and you want to be filled and empowered by the Spirit.

The Holy Spirit

God's love has been poured out into our hearts through the Holy Spirit, who has been given to us.

Romans 5:5

But the Advocate, the Holy Spirit, whom the Father will send in my name, will teach you all things and will remind you of everything I have said to you.

John 14:26

In the same way, the Spirit helps us in our weakness. We do not know what we ought to pray for, but the Spirit himself intercedes for us through wordless groans. And He who searches our hearts knows the mind of the Spirit, because the Spirit intercedes for God's people in accordance with the will of God.

Romans 8:26, 27

Forgiveness Instead of Resentment

Resentment and anger are likely to intensify anxiety. The good news is that this can be resolved through forgiveness.

Have you been holding a grudge against someone who has offended you? Don't delay in choosing to forgive! This will bring spiritual renewal and peace into your life. Ask God to show you the names of people you need to forgive, then make a list!

Why should you forgive others?

- Because God has forgiven you Ephesians 4:32
- Because God requires you to forgive Mark 11:25
- Because not forgiving provides an opportunity for Satan to take advantage of you 2 Corinthians 2:10, 11
- Because it improves health and relationships

What is forgiveness all about?

- It is a decision, not based on how you feel
- It does not minimize or condone what happened
- It is choosing to accept the painful consequences
- It is not about confronting the offender
- It is deciding to "let it go" - to not hold onto the offenses and the anger, or to seek revenge

Praying through Forgiveness

Lord, because You have forgiven me, I choose to forgive

______(name the person)______________________________

for ___(mention what this person has said or done____

______that was hurtful)______________________________.

I have experienced the difficult consequences of

___(what happened as a result)________________________

and I have felt ______(rejected, blamed, etc.)__________.

Lord, I release this person to You and ask You to bless him/her. Please forgive me for resentments I have held. I choose not to continue holding on to any anger or bitterness. Please heal my painful emotions. Amen

- Keep in mind that you *do not contact* the person you have forgiven to let them know about it. They tend to receive it as blame. Instead pray for the person and show kindness.
- Chapter 11 of *Victory Over the Darkness* has teaching on forgiveness. In *Steps to Freedom* there is more on forgiving and living in forgiveness.

Reset to Thankfulness

At times when technology does not work, someone says, "Press the reset button." Switching to thankfulness is like pressing the reset button of our minds. Can fear and worry survive when we have our minds focused on things to be thankful for? Not easily!

It's interesting to note how often the Apostle Paul mentions thankfulness. There must be a reason. The attitude of thankfulness brings calmness to our hearts and minds. It overcomes worry. It's that simple! Our dear friend Elsie once said, "Don't you think that the principles of scripture are really very simple?" Agreed!

God's teachings are profound but no university degree is needed to understand them and put them to work in our lives. So be thankful for life, for food, for friends and even for the hard things. In every circumstance, keep your thoughts on things to be thankful for.

> The unfolding of your words gives light;
> it gives understanding to the simple.
> Psalm 119:130

Do not be anxious about anything,
but in every situation,
by prayer and petition,
with **thanksgiving**,
present your requests to God.

And the peace of God,
which transcends all understanding,
will guard your hearts and your minds
in Christ Jesus.

Philippians 4:6, 7

What do You Feed Your Mind?

What you put into your mind will have an influence on your emotional well-being. When you watch a golden sunset you feel good. If you see a scary movie you may have a nightmare.

What do you *watch* or *listen to* or *play* that stirs up guilt, fear, worry or anxiety? If your conscience is tuned to biblical standards, and it should be, then immoral songs and scenes will raise guilt which increases anxiety. Documentaries or news casts provide much information, but may raise your level of fear and anxiety. Many games involve violence and the occult and are also a way of raising anxiety.

As you *play*, as you *watch*, as you *listen*, ask yourself important questions:

- Is this good for my spiritual well-being?
- Is this good for my emotional well-being?

Let your choices and decisions be guided by biblical principles and by the still small voice of the Holy Spirit who wants what is best for you.

I will set before my eyes no vile thing!

Psalm 101:3

The verse above was posted over the television in our host home in St. John's Newfoundland. Mel and Mary said they chose it to set a standard for television viewing for themselves and their children.

Finally, brothers and sisters,
whatever is true,
whatever is noble,
whatever is right,
whatever is pure,
whatever is lovely,
whatever is admirable –
if anything is excellent or praiseworthy –
think about such things.

Philippians 4:8

Surrender

When a preacher challenges us to surrender to Jesus we immediately fear that God will ask us to do something we don't want to do. Sound familiar?

- Surrender is an act of trusting in God.
- Surrender is putting the details of your life into God's hands which means there is nothing to worry about.
- Surrender is making Jesus the Lord of your life. It is a daily challenge and privilege.

Ask God to show you what you have not yet surrendered to Him ______(make a list)______.

Loving God, I confess that there have been fears and worries in my life because of things I have not fully given over to You. I ask your forgiveness for my lack of submission. I now surrender all these things to You

______(name them)______________________________.

I choose to trust You with each aspect of my past, present and future. I proclaim You as my Lord. In the name of Jesus Christ. Amen

I Surrender All

All to Jesus I surrender,
All to him I freely give;
I will ever love and trust him,
In his presence daily live.

All to Jesus I surrender,
Lord, I give myself to Thee;
Fill me with Thy love and power,
Let Thy blessing fall on me.

I surrender all. I surrender all.
All to thee, my blessed Saviour,
I surrender all. [31]

Judson W. Van DeVenter, 1896

Don't Go It Alone

We all like to manage on our own, like the 2-year-old needing help with a zipper but announcing loudly, "I do it 'self!"

The truth is, we need each other. God has designed us for community. In community there is love, care and encouragement.

Maybe you have been hurt by others and are scared to go to church or to be in a Bible Study group.

Yes, there are risks, as with all things in life. Every time we get into the car to go somewhere we could have an accident. Someone even said with tongue-in-cheek, "Don't go to bed because most people die in bed!"

Rather than staying away from church and fellowship, forgive those who have wounded you and go with the intention of being a blessing to others. Go with a prayer, "Oh God, speak to my heart today."

Fellowship

Neil Anderson and Rich Miller in *Freedom from Fear*

Encouragement is a great need for people struggling with fear and anxiety. Much of life in this world discourages us or takes courage out of us. To put courage in, God has given us each other. No congregation is perfect, but God is, and He delights to work through imperfect people. Neglecting fellowship with other Christians makes us greatly susceptible to having our hearts hardened by sin's deceitfulness and we are at risk of falling away from the living God. [32]

Tearing Down Strongholds

What is a spiritual stronghold? Paul refers to it in 2 Corinthians 10:3-5 as something that needs to be demolished.

Here is a definition, adapted from youth speaker Dave Park:

> A *stronghold* is being stuck in wrong behaviour patterns or wrong thoughts. Often this includes a sense of hopelessness about overcoming the negative patterns. [33]

The strongholds of worry and anxiety can be overcome with spiritual weapons such as the ones listed in Ephesians chapter 6. One of those powerful weapons is to have your mind filled with scripture. That would be the belt of truth, verse 14. Another weapon is to speak out the Word of God against any spiritual attack. That would be the sword of the Spirit, mentioned in verse 17. So, use your God-given armour to overcome anxiety and fear.

For though we live in the world,
we do not wage war as the world does.
The weapons we fight with
are not the weapons of the world.
On the contrary, they have divine power
to demolish *strongholds.*
We demolish arguments
and every pretension
that sets itself up
against the knowledge of God,
and we take captive every thought
to make it obedient to Christ.

2 Corinthians 10:3-5

34

Overcoming Oppression

story by Carolee

When I was a young mom with two small children we had someone staying at our home for a few months. Unknown to us, this person was involved with occult practices related to traditional religion. Gradually we noticed an oppressive atmosphere in our home, though we could not understand why.

The spiritual darkness became so great that I was overwhelmed with fear in our house and it was particularly acute when my husband was not home. At times it was hard to walk from one room into another. I discovered that when I spoke scriptures out loud and trusted in God's protection I was able to move about the house more freely.

One night Ken and I were very aware of a spiritual attack and both of us were desperate for relief from the oppression. We started talking about what Jesus did when evil spirits were afflicting someone. According to the gospels, He cast them out. He sent them away. We had no idea how to do that.

In the middle of the night we went out on our yard and in a stumbling way we followed the model of Jesus. We knew immediately that something had changed. Our property and our home became a safe and peaceful place.

We learned that speaking in the name of Jesus Christ will deliver us when we are attacked by fear.

> Be strong in the Lord and in his mighty power. Put on the full armour of God, so that you can take your stand against the devil's schemes. For our struggle is not against flesh and blood, but against the rulers, against the authorities, against the powers of this dark world and against the spiritual forces of evil in the heavenly realm.
>
> Ephesians 6:10-12

Simple Prescription from "Dr." James

James 4:7 and 8 has a prescription for winning a spiritual battle. Simple but not necessarily easy. There are three distinct parts.

- Turn to God and say YES to him
  (*submit* yourself to Him)
- Turn to Satan and say NO to him
  (*resist* the devil,
  in the name of Jesus Christ, of course)
- Turn back to God and draw near to him
  (*renew* your mind with scripture,
  songs, prayer, etc.)

Submit⇨Resist⇨Renew S⇨R⇨R

It is important to renounce the work of the evil one. However, that should *not* be our preoccupation or focus. Notice that the beginning and the end of the "prescription" is about connecting with God. That is where we should be focused. The result? We experience the presence and peace of Jesus!

On the following pages there are four examples of how to put James 4:7, 8 into practice.

Submit yourselves, then,

to God.

Resist the devil,

and he will flee from you.

Come near to God

and He will come near to you.

James 4:7, 8

Four Ways to Apply James 4:7-8

Example 1

I am a child of God.

In the name of Jesus Christ,

I stand against the fear that is now overwhelming me

________(name the fear)________.

The truth is ____(claim a scripture truth)____.

Example 2

Heavenly Father,

I submit my body and my mind to You.

In the name of Jesus Christ I resist the fear of ____

________(name it)________.

The truth is ____(state an encouraging truth

____from the Bible)____.

Example 3

I am a child of God and I submit myself to him. In the name of Jesus Christ I renounce this fear (OR temptation/ deception/ lie/ anxiety/ attack)

_________(name it)________________________.

I embrace the truth of God's Word __(name it)___.

Example 4

Heavenly Father,

I submit my mind and body to You.

In the name of Jesus Christ, I command Satan to leave me. I renounce the strategies and lies of Satan, including ___(name them)____________________.

The truth is that "the One who is in [me] is greater than the one who is in the world." 1 John 4:4

Prayer Path

Steps to Freedom is a way of committing every area of life to Jesus Christ. It is a prayer path for overcoming spiritual strongholds. A mature Christian, trained as a facilitator, helps another believer work through spiritual concerns, including –

- involvement in the occult, false religions
- negative thoughts, defense mechanisms
- fear, perfectionism, legalism, driveness
- self-harm, suicidal tendencies
- woundedness, offenses, bitterness
- negative perceptions of God
- rebellion, pridefulness
- complaining, arguing, criticising
- sexual sins, addictive behaviours
- generational patterns, spiritual oppression

The event includes the support of a prayer partner. Each of the steps involves confessing and renouncing sin and then submitting to God. *The goal is to walk in freedom.*

Search me O God

and know my heart.

Test me and know my anxious thoughts.

See if there is any offensive way in me,

and lead me in the way everlasting.

Psalm 139:23, 24

Steps to Freedom, Not for me!

For some people, the prospect of doing Steps to Freedom is terrifying. Before turning your back on the idea, ask yourself, could there be past experiences that contribute to anxiety? Yes, and God wants to bring healing to you. Could there be spiritual stuff in your life that contributes to anxiety? Yes! And God will give you the courage to face it.

If you are very sick, but you are afraid of doctors, would you still make an appointment and see a doctor? Probably! It would be wise to do so.

If surgery was the only way to get rid of a tumour, would you refuse surgery because you dread it? Probably not! And it would be wise to have the surgery.

It's always best to face your past and your problems, even if it temporarily increases your anxiety. God brings healing as you become honest and vulnerable before him.

Steps to Freedom, Yes I need that!

Are you wanting to go through Steps to Freedom? It is important to prepare yourself.

- Read *Victory Over the Darkness* and *The Bondage Breaker*
- *OR* read *Freedom from Fear*
- *OR* watch a DVD series with this teaching [35]

The Steps to Freedom can be found at the end of *The Bondage Breaker.* [36] However, there are expanded versions of Steps to Freedom available in workbook format and these are more convenient to use. The Steps to Freedom guide also contains useful resources for living in freedom.

There is a network of people around the world willing to take others through Steps to Freedom.

For books, DVDs and guides you may contact:

Living Free Ministries
livingfree@mts.net

A Story about Steps to Freedom

Should I marry this guy?

Ella was enjoying the company of Seth, a fine Christian young man. As time went on she found herself plagued with anxiety about whether she should marry him. She worried about what her friends and family thought of their relationship.

Doubt and anxiety had been with her for a long time. Guilt and self-blame were eroding her joy. When she felt overwhelmed she would notice that her breathing was very shallow.

Several people suggested to Ella that she should go through Steps to Freedom so she made an appointment to talk about the possibility. Soon after that she decided to do the required preparation and find a prayer partner. She was hoping desperately to find peace in her heart and clarity about marriage.

Ella found that after going through Steps to Freedom her ability to cope with life improved remarkably. Forgiving those who had offended her was a big step in reducing her anxiety. And she prayerfully decided to marry Seth.

For a while Ella felt like she was on an emotional honeymoon. But honeymoons come to an end and that's when she realized that she needed to make disciplined changes in her life. As she read the Bible and applied the truths, she found herself making steady progress in overcoming anxiety.

Then several unexpected circumstances burst into her life. Ella was very thankful that she had prayed through the seven steps and had found healing. It provided the foundation she needed to face the new challenges.

Ella is tackling difficult things with the encouragement of a godly husband and with hope in her heart. Praise and worship has been an important key for her in overcoming anxiety. She also finds the *Evening Prayer* very helpful. *(See next page.)* When things are hard she takes long slow breaths and reminds herself that it's not about her emotions; it's about taking the time to find her peace in God.

37

Evening Prayer

Heavenly Father, thank you that You brought me into your family and blessed me with every spiritual blessing in Christ Jesus. Thank you for this time of renewal and refreshment through sleep. I trust You to guard my mind and my body as I sleep.

I confess my sins of this day ____(name them)________ *and ask You to forgive me. I thank You that the blood of Jesus Christ cleanses me from all unrighteousness.*

Lord, in your strength I resist all the things that would interfere with the rest that You intend for me. I choose not to review my sins and mistakes because You have forgiven me. I choose to forgive anyone who has offended me and anyone who disturbs my sleep. I renounce all negative, selfish, sinful and resentful thoughts. I choose not to spend nighttime in planning and so be robbed of sleep. I choose instead to meditate on your Word and rest in You.

I renounce all fear and I cast my anxieties on You. Lord, please guard my mind from nightmares. I ask for your protection from every attempt of Satan and his demons to attack me during sleep. May your peace be in this place.

I submit my body to You as a living sacrifice and ask You to provide wholeness and healing. On the basis of my authority in Christ, I stand against the attacks of the enemy on any area of my life – physical, emotional, mental or spiritual. I commit myself to You, God, as my Provider, my Healer and my Protector.

In the strong name of the Lord Jesus Christ. Amen [38]

Adapted from the Evening Prayer in *Steps to Freedom*

39

May the God of hope
fill you with all joy and peace
as you trust in him,
so that you
may overflow with hope
by the power of the Holy Spirit.

Romans 15:13

PRAYERS

For Overcoming Worry, Fear and Anxiety

Digging Deeper

Here is an opportunity to pray through your worries and anxieties. Facing fears is not easy but it is necessary in order to overcome them. In this final section of the book there is a guide for praying. It is best to do it with the support of a mature Christian.

Prayer

Heavenly Father, I choose to face my fears and anxieties in the power of the Holy Spirit.
In the strong name of Jesus Christ. Amen

> God has not given us a spirit of fear, but of power and of love and of a sound mind.
> 2 Timothy 1:7 NKJV

I prayed to the Lord, and He answered me.
He freed me from all my fears.
Those who look to him for help
  will be radiant with joy;
  no shadow of shame will darken their faces.
In my desperation I prayed,
  and the Lord listened;
He saved me from all my troubles
  for the angel of the Lord is a guard.
He surrounds and defends all who fear him.

Psalm 34:4-7 NLT

Your Story

We all have a story, many stories, many chapters of life. Your story holds clues to why you are worried and anxious. When facing your fears, it is important to first reflect on your life and its many chapters.

Lord, as I seek to uncover the roots of anxiety in my life,
I ask You to show me what I need to be aware of.
In the name of Jesus I pray. Amen

Read the next page, then take time to consider your life and where anxiety may have started. Make a few notes.

- family of origin
- childhood and home life
- adolescence
- young adulthood
- community, church, work, career
- singleness, marriage, family, sexuality
- involvement in the occult or false religion
- health problems, addiction, trauma, other

A Life Line

As you think about your personal story or your fears, you may have a sudden feeling of fear or panic.

JESUS is your place of safety! Take refuge in him.

Here is one way to do that –
Recall a time when you felt close to God, a specific *place* and *time* when you felt God's encouragement or nearness. *Rest* in that memory. Then *write* it down or share it with someone. Return to that memory often as you recall difficult things in your life.

Here is a personalized version of Zephaniah 3:17

The Lord my God is with me;
He is mighty to save.
He takes great delight in me,
He quiets me with his love,
He rejoices over me with singing.[40]

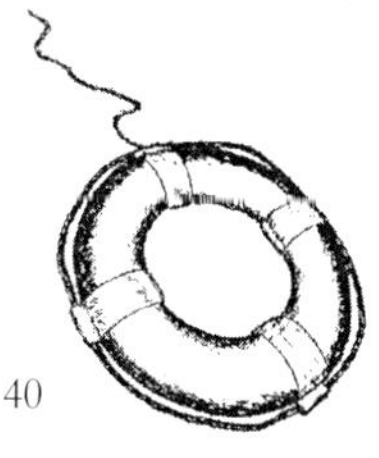
[41]

Facing Your Fears

Your story has brought many things to mind. Are you willing to ask God to show you areas where you need to confess, repent, renounce and submit?

Heavenly Father, I desire your peace and freedom in my life. Instead of trusting in You I have allowed fear, worry and anxiety to fill my thoughts.

I ask You to reveal to me all the fears and lies that have been controlling me so that I can confess and renounce each one with the help of the Holy Spirit. Lord, show me the wrong attitudes and behaviours that are connected to my anxiety or contribute to it, so that I can confess and turn away from all that prevents me from living in freedom.

I ask You to protect me from the attacks of the evil one as I do this. In the powerful name of Jesus Christ I pray. Amen

In a column on a separate page list the anxieties and fears that the Holy Spirit brings to your mind: ____

____

The Lies We Believe

Most of our fears have lies associated with them. The trouble is, they seem logical and we don't even realize that we are living with a deception. In the fears listed below, notice the lies that may be connected to them.

- *fear* of losing a job: *thinking* it would be impossible to find other employment
- *fear* of moving: *thinking* I won't have any friends
- *fear* of disapproval: *thinking* that my self-worth depends on people approving of me
- *fear* of making decisions: *thinking* that I will make a mistake and have a bad outcome
- *fear* of losing salvation: *thinking* I have committed a sin that God won't forgive

Next to the fears you listed (see previous page), write down the related lies. If this is hard to do, don't become anxious; simply ask God to bring to your mind what you need to know. Then continue on in the next pages. You will have the opportunity to confess fears and lies when you get to pages 150-151.

Begin choosing verses that counteract each fear.

Negative Thoughts

Anxiety thrives on negative thoughts and attitudes. Negativity is a hotbed where fears and worries sprout easily. Many of our negative thoughts are deceptions about ourselves, about life and about God.

Ask God to reveal any wrong thinking that has become part of your life. As the Holy Spirit brings things to your attention, write them down.

Here are a few common negative thoughts

- thinking that I am not of value
- thinking I have to be perfect
- thinking that I have to be or feel in control
- thinking something bad is going to happen
- thinking that God is distant and disinterested
- thinking God won't come through for me
- thinking God is holding my past against me

Beside each item on your list put two or three scripture truths that counteract the negative thought.

Prayer

Lord, I confess and repent of my negative thoughts and wrong attitudes about myself, about life and about You. I have been thinking that ____(name one negative ____thought at a time)____.

Instead I choose the truth from your Word which is ________________.

Heavenly Father, I renounce these negative and wrong patterns and receive your forgiveness and cleansing. I commit myself to filling my mind with true and uplifting thoughts so that I will be able to overcome anxiety. I choose to believe that you are a loving Father and I affirm that in You I am accepted, secure and deeply significant. In the name of Jesus Christ. Amen

> Be made new in the attitude of your minds.
> Ephesians 4:23

Self-Protective Behaviours

When we are anxious we tend to develop coping behaviours in an attempt to ease our anxiety. The trouble is that as time goes along they work against us. These self-protective behaviours may be irresponsible, may damage relationships and often have other bad consequences. They also keep us from being a good witness for Jesus.

What behaviours in your life are linked to fear, worry and anxiety? Below are some common ones. Ask God to show you what coping behaviours you use.

Avoiding
procrastinating, withdrawing, not sharing feelings, avoiding certain people or certain circumstances, not making decisions, isolating

Escaping, medicating, comforting
drinking, drugs, smoking, unhealthy eating, using pornography, wrong sexual thoughts or activities, workaholism, gambling, over-spending, being overly occupied with gaming, texting, social media, movies, fitness, etc.

Prayer

Lord, I confess I have reacted to anxiety by trying to protect myself in various ways, including ___________

____

____.

Heavenly Father, I ask your forgiveness and I renounce these self-protective patterns. I now commit myself to facing my past, my problems and my anxieties with your help. You are my Rock, my Deliverer and my Refuge. In the name of Jesus Christ. Amen

Write out Bible verses that will assure you of God's presence and protection; for example Psalm 3:3, 9:9, 18:2, 27:5, 32:7.

Note: If you are struggling with an addictive or destructive behaviour, you should seek further spiritual and professional help.

Praying Through Fears and Anxieties

- As you prepare to pray, go back to your list of fears (see p 142) and choose one worry, fear or anxiety to start with.
- Using the guide on the next pages, write or type out your prayer step by step.
- Be thoughtful in choosing an Anchor Verse that will strengthen you.
- After you have written out all the parts of the prayer, go on to another worry, fear or anxiety.
- After you have prepared about three, meet with a mature Christian for encouragement and support as you pray through them out loud. In James 5:16 we read that healing comes when we break the silence and confess before others.
- Write your Anchor Verse(s) on separate cards and repeat them often to renew your mind.

A Challenge

From *Freedom From Fear*

Facing our fears
is one of the toughest things we do,
but God has promised
to walk with us through it. [42]

We need to stop submitting to fear
and start submitting to God. [43]

Praying About Fears

Rely on the Holy Spirit to help you as you pray.

1. *Lord, I confess and repent of the fear of*

   ____

2. *The physical symptoms I have noticed are*

   ____

3. *This fear started when* ________________________

   ____

4. *I have believed the lie that* ____________________

   ____

5. *I renounce this fear and the lies connected to it and choose to believe the truth that* ________________

   ______(choose at least one scripture verse)______

   ____

6. *I also confess the ways this fear is connected to negative thoughts and attitudes such as (p 144-145)*

____

____

and to self-protective behaviours such as (p 146-147)

____

____.

7. *Lord, I choose to live by faith in You. I believe the promises of your Word that You will be with me and help me no matter what happens. Amen*

Declaration

In the powerful name of Jesus Christ, I renounce any spirit of fear. As a child of God I stand against all strategies of Satan that overwhelm me or in any other way prevent me from overcoming my fears. I receive the freedom that God offers me.

Affirmations, Part One

Speak them out loud with conviction.

I declare that I am a child of God. John 1:12

I bring all my concerns to God and in exchange I receive his peace. Isaiah 26:3; Philippians 4:6, 7

I choose to dwell on what is "true, noble, right, pure, lovely, and admirable." Philippians 4:8

I affirm that I am free forever from condemnation. Romans 8:1, 2

The truth is that I am hidden with Christ in God. Colossians 3:3

I reject all fear and choose to walk by faith in the power of the Holy Spirit. Psalm 27:1

I trust in God who is with me no matter what happens. Daniel 3:17, 18; John 16:33

I am assured that all things work together for good to those who love God. Romans 8:28

Affirmations, Part Two

I renounce Satan's lies and embrace God's truth so that I will be set free of fear. John 8:31, 32

The truth is that God will strengthen me, help me and uphold me. Isaiah 41:10

I affirm that I cannot be separated from the love of God. Romans 8:35-39

The truth is that I am born of God and the evil one cannot touch me. 1 John 5:18

I command Satan by the authority I have in Jesus Christ to leave my presence. 2 Corinthians 10:3-5

I commit myself to rejoice in the Lord daily. Psalm 63:3, 4; Philippians 4:4; 1 Thessalonians 5:16

I am confident that the good work God has begun in me will be perfected. Philippians 1:6

Affirmations, Part Three

I submit myself to Jesus as Lord. James 4:7

I resist Satan and all his evil workers in the name of Jesus Christ. James 4:7; I Peter 5:8, 9

The truth is that Satan is already defeated by Jesus on the cross. 1 Corinthians 15:57

I choose to place my confidence in God. Psalm 56:3, 4; Psalm 4:8; Psalm 89:18; Romans 8:28

I renounce any spirit of fear in the powerful name of Jesus Christ. 2 Timothy 1:7

The truth is that I can find grace and mercy to help in time of need. Hebrews 4:16

I cast all my anxieties on God. 1 Peter 5:7

I choose to live with an attitude of thankfulness in all circumstances. Philippians 4:4-7, 1 Thessalonians 5:18

I declare that God has not given me a spirit of fear, but of power, love and a sound mind. 2 Timothy 1:7

Stay alert!
  Watch out for your great enemy, the devil.
He prowls around like a roaring lion,
  looking for someone to devour.
Stand firm against him,
  and be strong in your faith.
Remember that your family of believers
  all over the world
  is going through
  the same kind of suffering you are.

1 Peter 5:8, 9 NLT

Overcoming Anxiety from Day to Day

walking in freedom

- The Anchor Verses will continue to establish you in the promises and encouragement of God's Word. Soak yourself in them!
- Review the prayers for facing your fears. Affirm them out loud.
- Speak out a page of the Affirmations as part of your morning routine or your daily prayer time.
- Rely on the power of the Holy Spirit for changing your thoughts, attitudes and behaviours.

You will find that new fears arise when there are new circumstances, new challenges and new stages in life. When you become aware of a new fear, choose to trust God. Use the preceding pages to pray about it.

As you trust God, the Holy Spirit will transform your life. Dynamic things happen when God's people follow God's Word and God's ways.

We would like to hear how you are overcoming worry, fear and anxiety as a result of reading and using this book. Contact us at livingfree@mts.net.

Perseverance

from *Freedom From Fear*

It takes time
to overcome phobias
and deep-seated anxieties.

You will be tempted to think
the battle is too hard
and not worth the effort.

Those are the times
when you need perseverance
and encouragement
to not give up. [44]

Concluding Prayer

Heavenly Father, You are loving and You are powerful and so I choose to put my trust in You as my Saviour, my Protector and my Provider.

Thank you for helping me to face up to fear in my life. I ask You to fill me with the Holy Spirit so that, in your strength, I can live a godly and responsible life.

In the strong name of Jesus Christ I pray. Amen

The Lord bless you and keep you;

the Lord make his face
to shine upon you,
and be gracious to you;
the Lord lift up his countenance
upon you,
and give you peace. [45]

Amen

The grace of our Lord Jesus Christ
be with you!

Honouring Our Heroes!

by Ken

Shortly after Neil Anderson founded Freedom in Christ, Carolee and I had the privilege of meeting him. He was presenting a seminar which we attended. As a result of that event we began taking people through Steps to Freedom and later joined the staff of Freedom in Christ. We had supporting roles in the seminars that he offered in Delta, British Columbia; Winnipeg, Manitoba and Moncton, New Brunswick. After that, we presented his video seminar about 40 times across Canada, gradually beginning to teach the sessions ourselves. When people come to us with their spiritual and personal concerns we use tools gained from FIC as well as many years of pastoral work. We feel that our prayer ministry has been significantly shaped by the teaching and example of Neil Anderson. Presently he is active in ministry as well as daily spending time with his wife who is in a health care facility. Out of this experience has come his recent book, *The Power of Presence – A Love Story*. Neil Anderson has had a big impact on our lives.

Rich Miller is the second person that we want to honour. I first got to know him in Colorado when I attended his workshop at a large Freedom in Christ event. Rich was telling the story of a teen who had many negative thoughts about God. On the screen was the *Truth about our Heavenly Father* [46] which listed a biblical truth to counter each negative thought about God. I was busy scribbling notes, when I heard someone sobbing, and then realized it was me. Even after decades of ministry I struggled with feeling that God was distant and passive. Rich stopped teaching and walked over to me, knelt down and placed his hand on my knee and prayed silently. After a while I regained composure and Rich continued teaching. I was impressed that even when he was leading a workshop he took the time to care for one person. Rich is now the president of Freedom in Christ Ministries, USA.

Thank you Neil and Rich for your influence in our lives.

Ken

Recommended Reading

From Dr. Neil T. Anderson

Victory Over the Darkness

- our identity in Christ
- winning the battle for the mind
- healing emotional wounds

The Bondage Breaker

- understanding spiritual warfare
- breaking stubborn habits and secret sins

Freedom From Fear

Dr. Neil T. Anderson and Rich Miller

- overcoming anxious thoughts with truth
- casting all our anxieties on Christ

Bibliography

Anderson, Neil T., *The Bondage Breaker.* Oregon: Harvest House Publishers, 1990/2000.

Anderson, Neil T., *Victory Over the Darkness.* Minneapolis: Bethany House, 1990/2000/2013.

Anderson, Neil T. and Rich Miller, *Freedom From Fear, Overcoming Worry and Anxiety.* Oregon: Harvest House Publishers, 1999.

Jeremiah, David, *What are You Afraid Of? Facing Down Your Fears with Faith.* Illinois: Tyndale House, 2013.

Leaf, Caroline, *Switch on Your Brain, The Key to Peak Happiness, Thinking and Health.* Grand Rapids: Baker Books, 2013.

Note: The *Steps to Freedom* guide is available through Living Free Ministries livingfree@mts.net

End Notes

[1] Open Bible, sketch by Ken. This symbol highlights some of the places where Bible verses are featured.

[2] Neil T. Anderson and Rich Miller, *Freedom from Fear, Overcoming Worry and Anxiety* (Eugene, Oregon: Harvest House Publishers, 1999), 13.

[3] David Jeremiah, *What are You Afraid Of, Facing Down Your Fears with Faith* (Carol Stream, Illinois: Tyndale House Publishers, Inc., 2013), xi.

[4] Ibid., xii.

[5] Musical notes, sketch by Ken. The image gives a visual indication that a song is featured.

[6] In 1855 Joseph M. Scriven received news from Ireland of his mother being very ill. He wrote a poem to comfort her and it later became the hymn "What a Friend We Have in Jesus."

[7] Joy Banks gave permission to include an image of one of her lino prints. Joy lives in Vancouver, British Columbia and serves on the pastoral team of Grandview Calvary Baptist Church.

[8] Priscilla Owens (1829–1907) wrote "We have an Anchor" for her Sunday School students at the Union Square Methodist Episcopal Church in Baltimore, Maryland.

[9] Anchor, sketch by Ken. The anchor is used as a theme throughout the book. It is also used on the edge of pages, to indicate a section of Anchor Verses.

[10] Jennifer Benson Schuldt, *Our Daily Bread®,* © 2016 by Our Daily Bread Ministries, Grand Rapids, MI. Reprinted by permission. All rights reserved. This devotional appeared in print on November 1, 2016.

[11] Caroline Leaf, *Switch on Your Brain, the Key to Peak Happiness, Thinking and Health* (Grand Rapids, Michigan: Baker Books, 2013), 76.

[12] Ibid., 72.

[13] Ibid., 163.

[14] Neil T. Anderson, *The Bondage Breaker* (Eugene, Oregon: Harvest House Publishers, 2000), 216.

[15] "Standing on the Promises" was written in 1886 by Russell Kelso Carter.

[16] Connie Smith, ©2000 Steadfast Music Services, used with permission. Connie is a friend whose life has demonstrated that renewing the mind will have an impact in a person's relationships and circumstances.

[17] For 20 years we have used the cottage of our friend, Ed Redekopp, at Arnes, Manitoba, on Lake Winnipeg. In the cottage hung a small plaque, picturing two birds having a conversation. The poem reminded us of the simple trust that we should have in God.

[18] The Anchor Verses can be obtained in 5.5x8.5 and 8.5x11 formats. See the blog of Living Free Ministries: https://livingfreeministries-wpg.blogspot.ca/p/anchor-verses.html The links at the top of the page lead to the PDF documents.

[19] "Turn Your Eyes Upon Jesus" is a hymn that has given focus to many believers when the storms of life have caused fear. When the disciple Peter (Matthew 14:22-36) noticed the force of wind and waves, he began to sink into the sea because he had taken his eyes off Jesus. He cried out and Jesus saved him. Hebrews 12:2 says, "Let us fix our eyes on Jesus."

[20] Kate Wilkinson wrote, "May the word of God dwell richly in my heart from hour to hour; so that all may see I triumph only through his power." The words of this popular hymn have challenged many Christ-followers to depend on God.

[21] Leaf, *"Switch on Your Brain,"* 85. "Research shows that when we don't engage in this disciplined and focused self-reflective pattern of thinking that activates the DMN, we may experience negative self-esteem, depression, worry, anxiety, and health issues.... We may get stuck, unable to cope, and have a tendency to focus on the problem and not the solution."

[22] Adapted from the 21-Day Brain Detox Plan developed by Dr. Caroline Leaf. A modest subscription fee will entitle you to use this plan repeatedly over a one-year period: http://21daybraindetox.com/

[23] Steve Goss, Director of Freedom in Christ International, teaches *Stronghold Busting*. It consists of the following:

a. Determine the lie you have been believing

b. Write down what effects believing the lie has had on your life

c. Find Bible verses that state the truth and write them down

d. Write a prayer or declaration based on the formula:

I renounce the lie that...

I announce the truth that...

e. Read the Bible verses and say the prayer/declaration every day for forty days.

For more information and helpful examples, see *Freedom in Christ Discipleship Course, Participant Guide* (Grand Rapids, Michigan: Monarch Books, 2009), 80-86.

[24] Ibid., 133.

[25] Ibid., 151.

[26] John Neufeld, The Meeting Place post. November 17, 2014 at 11:47 am. See also http://www.themeetingplace.mb.ca/

[27] Neil T. Anderson, *Victory Over the Darkness* (Bloomington, Minnesota: Bethany House Publishers, 2013), 24.

[28] Ibid, 38, 39.

[29] A declaration is NOT a prayer. It is a strong statement or a formal assertion.

[30] The prayer for assurance and the declaration are adapted from materials by Dr. Neil T. Anderson.

[31] Dr. Billy Graham, described Mr. Van DeVenter, the writer of "I Surrender All," as "one of the evangelists who influenced my early preaching." When Billy Graham attended Florida Bible Institute (now Trinity Bible College) in the late 1930s, the students would gather at the home of Mr. Van DeVenter for fellowship. The song, "I Surrender All," was often used in the Billy Graham Crusades. https://en.wikipedia.org/wiki/I_Surrender_All

[32] Anderson and Miller, *Freedom from Fear*, 231.

[33] Dave Park was formerly director of Freedom in Christ Youth Ministries. He has co-authored many books with Neil Anderson and is the speaker on the Busting Free video series. He is the founder of Infusion Ministries.

[34] Broken chain, sketch by Ken. The image is inspired by *The Bondage Breaker.* It is Jesus Christ that breaks the chains!

[35] There are DVD series with 10, 12 or 13 sessions. They can be obtained from Living Free Ministries or one of the national FIC offices.

[36] Anderson, *The Bondage Breaker*, "Steps to Freedom," 199-252.

[37] The "running man" was one of the early logos of Freedom in Christ. It is rarely used now but has a powerful message as the runner breaks the tape in victory!

[38] Adapted from the Evening Prayer in "Steps to Freedom."

[39] Praying hands, sketch by Ken. The image is only used three times to highlight prayer.

[40] Zephaniah 3:17, personalized by Ken. "This verse was like a warm embrace for me one sunny, summer afternoon when I needed encouragement."

[41] Life ring, sketch by Ken. "I know from a traumatic experience what it is like to have a life ring tossed to me. A friend and I were rescued from certain death when we were far from shore in icy waters!"

[42] Anderson and Miller, *Freedom from Fear,* 205.

[43] Ibid., 190.

[44] Ibid., 271.

[45] "The Lord bless you and keep you…" is a well-known and much loved blessing. It is also referred to as a benediction. In Numbers 6:24-26 the Lord says to Moses, "This is how you are to bless the [people]."

[46] Heavenly Father page: found on pages 307-308 in *Freedom from Fear.* You may access the PDF and print it for your church or small group. https://livingfreeministries-wpg.blogspot.ca/p/anchor-verses.html

Index of Bible References